Raising Emotionally Healthy Kids

H. Norman Wright
Gary J. Oliver, Ph.D.

Formerly titled *Kids Have Feelings Too!*

VICTOR BOOKS

A DIVISION OF SCRIPTURE PRESS PUBLICATIONS INC.
USA CANADA ENGLAND

Copyediting: Linda Holland
Cover design: Grace Chan Mallette

Library of Congress Cataloging-in-Publication Data

Wright, H. Norman.
    [Kids have feelings too]
    Raising emotionally healthy kids / H. Norman Wright, Gary J. Oliver.
        p.   cm.
    Originally published : Kids have feelings too. © 1993.
    Includes bibliographical references.
    ISBN 1-56476-451-6
    1. Family—Religious life. 2. Children—Religious life. 3. Emotions in children. 4. Emotions—Religious aspects—Christianity. 5. Parenting—Religious aspects—Christianity. I. Oliver, Gary. J. II. Title.
    BV4526.2.W735   1995
    248.8′45—dc20   94-41430
                                                                                          CIP

---

    2   3   4   5   6   7   8   9   10   Printing / Year   97   96   95

For information write Victor Books,
1825 College Avenue, Wheaton, Illinois 60187.

DEDICATION

To my daughter Sheryl Wright Macauley, and the memory of my son Matthew Norman Wright.

To my sons Nathan Jackson Oliver, Matthew David Oliver, and Andrew Michael Oliver.

You have been our wisest and best teachers. God has used you to give us a deeper understanding of our own emotions. We love you and thank God for you.

CONTENTS

INTRODUCTION

Few things are more important than our emotions. They are the warp and woof that determine the quality and significance of our lives. Each day we all experience a variety of feelings ranging from curiosity to surprise, from happiness to anger, from delight to despair — sometimes within moments of each other.

It's no exaggeration to say that our emotions influence every part of our lives. They are like a sixth sense, monitoring our needs, making us aware of good and evil, and providing motivation and energy for growth and change. Emotions give us the vigor and impetus for living. They help us understand ourselves and others, and warn us when we are in danger — when our boundaries are being crossed, or our rights are being violated. Emotions even help define our values. As go our emotions, so goes everything else in our lives.

God speaks to us through our emotions. The Bible has a lot to say about feelings. From Genesis through Revelation we read about God's emotions and those of the men, women, and children He created. According to Scripture, Christ experienced and expressed a wide range of feelings, including love, compassion, joy, fear, sorrow, disappointment, discouragement, frustration, hurt, rejection, loneliness, and anger.[1] When God created us in His image, He gave us a mind, a will, and emotions. Being human means we will experience emotions. They may be positive or negative, pleasurable or painful. We can acknowledge them or ignore them. We can learn to use our emotions constructively or allow them to control us. The only part that's optional is how we choose to express them.

In counseling, we work with adults who, as children, never learned to understand, value, and deal with their emotions. They have spent their entire lives struggling with and trying to overcome the consequences of unhealthy habits. Their emotional illiteracy has been a major contributor to a wide range of problems that complicate their lives.

Like the law of gravity, we may not always be aware of our emotions, but ignoring them can cause us serious problems. This is especially true with children. In fact, the main reason parents seek counseling for their children is because of emotional difficulties. Undetected, these difficulties may be disguised as performance problems in school, stomachaches, headaches, sleeping disorders, or poor behavior. But most often, at the core, they are emotional problems.

When we take the time to help our children understand their feelings, accept them, and express them in creative ways, we are doing them a big favor. The way children learn to handle their feelings is fundamental to how happy they will be as adults. If children learn to face fear, rebound from rejection, and grow through grief, they are more likely to become healthy adults. Regardless of age, we all know how it feels to be afraid or angry, happy or sad. Even my two-year-old son Andrew can tell the difference between these basic emotions. Whenever Carrie and I are having a disagreement, he'll point his little finger directly at us and say, "No, Mom. No, Dad." Of course, he doesn't understand his feelings, but he does know that a certain facial expression and tone of voice communicate something that is unpleasant to him.

The good news is that, with proper guidance and God's help, our children can begin right now to develop healthy emotional attitudes. As parents, we can communicate that in our family it is safe to experience and express feelings. We can give our kids a vocabulary for expressing what they feel and teach them to differentiate between experiencing and expressing emotions. And, we can set goals for their emotional growth that shape the kinds of habits they develop.

As counselors, we constantly get questions from Christian parents about how they can help their children understand and deal with their emotions and develop healthy response patterns. This book is a response to those questions. *Kids Have Feelings Too!* will give you a better understanding of the role emotions play in God's plan for you and your children. It will help you identify the unique personality of each child in your family and better understand his or her changing needs at various stages of development. In these pages you'll discover tools to help them grow toward healthy emotional maturity. In addition, we'll deal with several emotions that, in our experience, tend to be especially problematic to parents. In fact, the chapters in section two will focus on applying practical principles to these specific emotions.

Our ability to help our kids develop healthy emotional patterns is directly related to our own ability to model healthy emotions. Many of us grew up in homes that taught unbalanced, dysfunctional patterns. That's not a criticism of our parents—they modeled what they had learned as children. But many of us have unresolved issues that interrupted our emotional maturing. And, while our children bring us tremendous satisfaction, they can be a real source of frustration and discouragement. The greatest challenge we face may be dealing with our own responses to our children. So, as we discuss emotional attitudes throughout this book, we'll be dealing with our own development as well and in the final chapter, we'll discuss parents' emotional responses to their children.

As we identify and understand our own emotional habits, we can begin to modify old patterns and develop new ones that nurture our children and help them on their journey toward becoming emotionally healthy adults.

We can learn a lot about emotions by reflecting on our own experiences. Before going on, take a few minutes to think about the following questions:

- What is an emotion?
- What emotions do you frequently experience?
- What emotions are easy for you to express?
- What emotions are difficult for you to express?
- What emotions did you see expressed in your own family?
- What emotions were never expressed in your own family?
- Did you consider yourself emotionally narrow or broad?
- Have you ever had an emotion?

- When did you last experience an emotion?
- How long ago was it?
- Which emotion was it?
- What makes some emotions good and others bad?
- What makes some emotions desirable and others undesirable?

The role emotions play in God's plan for you and your children.

Identifying each of your children's unique personalities, and understanding their changing needs.

Understanding Healthy Emotional Response

If we are going to raise healthy kids — kids who become all that God designed and intended them to be — we must first understand what God meant in Genesis 1:16 when He said, "Let Us make man in Our image, according to Our likeness."

CREATED IN GOD'S IMAGE

The most unique aspect of being human is that we are made in the image of God. Because of sin, our God-image has been damaged and distorted, but we still bear resemblance to our Creator.

God designed us with a body, spirit, and soul. Many Christians understand and appreciate the importance of the body; our body is God's temple. Most Christians understand and appreciate the importance of the spirit; our spirit interacts and communes with God. Unfortunately, fewer Christians understand the soul. What comes to mind when you think of the word *soul*? How do you define it? We could accurately describe it as our personalities. It consists of our mind, will, and emotions. God created in us the ability to think, to choose, and to feel. All three are equally important.

GIVING VALIDITY TO OUR EMOTIONS

Many of us grew up in homes and churches that emphasized the mind and will, but denied the validity of emotions. More comfortable with facts than with feelings, our parents taught us that, if we think logically and make sound choices, we won't have to deal with our emotions. They will somehow take care of themselves. That philosophy has prejudiced us against our feelings. We have come to believe that they are not worthy of our attention, not to be trusted and, in fact, conflict with our faith.

Why is that? Maybe it's because we don't feel safe with our feelings. We've all seen or read about outrageous, horrible things that happened when people lost control of their emotions — acts done in the heat of anger, or during times of deep depression or grief.

THE MYTH OF GOOD AND BAD EMOTIONS

One of the myths many people have is that there are good and bad emotions. I have heard several sincere and well-intentioned speakers say that there are some emotions that should be cultivated and others that should be avoided at all cost. A key factor in this myth is the assumption that "good" Christians shouldn't have "bad" emotions. I've worked with adults who, as children, learned that certain emotions were good and certain ones were bad. Some were acceptable and others unacceptable. Worse yet, they learned that if they expressed the "negative" emotions, they themselves were unacceptable. This is not only erroneous but is also a potentially dangerous misconception.

In themselves, emotions aren't good or bad, right or wrong, healthy or unhealthy — they simply *are*. It's the way we learn to deal with our emotions that causes us problems. Emotional maturity involves learning to distinguish between experiencing the emotion and how we choose to express it. A feeling is one thing — expressing that feeling is another. This is an important distinction for adults to make, and one of the first things we want to teach our children.

The emotion of anger is a great example. Many Christians view anger as a negative emotion, and they work hard to repress, suppress, deny, and ignore it. That makes anger a very big problem. When we don't understand it and haven't learned effective ways to express it, anger can get out of control. When anger is out of control, it can have a devastating effect. Like other emotions, anger is energy. It is a source of power that can be used constructively or destructively. The energy can be directed in healthy or unhealthy ways. When properly understood, anger has tremendous potential for good.

The degree to which our emotions help or hinder us directly relates to our ability to acknowledge them, understand them, and channel them through a balanced, healthy perspective.

EMOTIONS CAN BE PLEASANT OR PAINFUL

One of the reasons people consider some emotions positive and others negative is because they can be experienced as both pleasant and painful. We automatically associate pleasant feelings with positive emotions, painful feelings with negative. Pleasant feelings provide a sense of safety and security. They tell a child that this situation is good and safe. These kinds of emotions cause children to seek out relationships, to trust, to be vulnerable, to risk rather than retreat, to be receptive rather than resistant.

Painful feelings can be a signal of impending danger, or a warning that something is wrong. Painful emotions put us on alert. They increase our awareness of what is going on around us. A child experiencing painful feelings may question his safety and tend to mistrust others. Fear motivates a child to hide, run, escape, or try to protect herself from something or someone. Anger provides the child with energy to take action and move from a defensive to an offensive position.

Another reason emotions have gotten a bad name is that they can be unreliable, inconsistent, and difficult to understand. They don't always make sense. At times we want to feel one way and end up feeling another. Also, most people I work with have experienced poor modeling—or none at all—and little biblical teaching about the place of emotions in the Christian life. They simply don't feel comfortable with their feelings.

I think one of the main reasons many people have become emotional invalids is because our emotions force us to look at our real selves, to see our humanity, our weaknesses, our vulnerabilities, our "dark" side. God speaks to us through our emotions, and we don't always like the message.

AN ISSUE OF BALANCE

Emotional maturity is like cement. For cement to do what it is designed to do, there must be a proper combination of cement, sand, and water. If the mixture is slightly off in its balance of ingredients, it will be weak. If you leave one ingredient out of your mixture, the cement will crumble.

Our personality requires a similar balance of ingredients. Because of sin, our soul's balance has been knocked askew, so we tend to respond in two unhealthy extremes. One way is to deny, repress, suppress, and ignore them. For those in this category, the heart can't be trusted—the mind is all that counts. The second unhealthy extreme is to let our emotions overwhelm and control us. In this case, the head can't be trusted—when in doubt, ignore the mind and go with your gut instinct. A healthy person is one who has learned to balance the mind, will, and emotions.

Dwight's Story

Dwight and Julie are good examples of the painful effects of growing up in homes where unhealthy responses were modeled. In Dwight's home, the man was the most important person in the house. His father Dean had all the power, was always right, and his needs came first. Independence was squelched, questions were discouraged, disagreements weren't allowed, and there was little open display of affection. The family's purpose was to compliment, honor, and obey Dad.

Theoretically, this was considered the biblical model for their family. In reality, though, the reason was so that Dad could feel good about himself.

Dean was the kind of father who needed successful kids who made him feel successful. He didn't mind if they expressed socially acceptable emotions that made him look and feel good. But he taught his kids to repress any negative emotions. He discouraged and punished them for expressing any emotion that communicated weakness or pain. He didn't know how to deal with these kinds of emotions and he thought they made the family look bad.

Dean's children learned that you shouldn't experience certain emotions. And, if you do, something is wrong with you—you are weak, inferior, a failure. If others find out you have these emotions, they will criticize, humiliate, and reject you. Never let someone of the opposite sex find out about the "real" you.

Imagine a young boy who grows up with this kind of modeling. He goes to college, falls in love with a delightful young woman, and gets married. With pressures of finishing college, finding a job, climbing the corporate ladder, and becoming a parent, he must face many new challenges and learn to make decisions on his own. His sense of competence and worth can easily become threatened.

That's exactly what happened to Dwight—he went to college, fell in love, and married Julie. Faced with new challenges, he responded the way he had been taught: he stuffed his fear, hid his worries, and denied his doubts. After all, he was the man and should instinctively know what to do. If he felt confused or discouraged, he wouldn't show it. He would pretend everything was fine, because if Julie found out how insecure and weak he really was, she would probably lose respect for him. She might even divorce him.

Julie's Story

Julie's childhood was very different from Dwight's. She grew up in a home where Dad was an alcoholic. When sober, he was a wonderful, sensitive father, but when he drank, he became unpredictable. She remembers as a child listening for him to come home from work. If the tires screeched as he drove in the driveway, she knew to stay out of the way. Whereas Dwight grew up in an emotionless home, Julie grew up in a home where expressions of emotion were inconsistent and out of control. At a young age, she learned that emotions couldn't be trusted.

Twenty-five years later Dwight and Julie came in for counseling. Dwight was burned out and close to a nervous breakdown. He dealt with his enormous fear by working longer and harder and medicating himself with alcohol. In time alcohol became his friend—it helped him deal with the struggles and complexities of his life.

Julie was also burned out. But, in her opinion, her problems stemmed from twenty-five years of struggle to have a relationship with someone who, as a child, had "relational bypass surgery." She loved Dwight deeply but, early in the marriage, she realized that he was incapable of intimacy. The warmth and emotional intensity he had expressed during their courtship had vanished in marriage.

When children came, Julie looked to her kids to fill the void in her life. She hoped and prayed Dwight would change, but as the years rolled by, they became married singles—they lived together, slept together, shared the same home, family, and friends. But they were strangers. Now with the children grown and leaving home, the reality of their relational bankruptcy could no longer be denied.

Millions of adults share similar experiences because their emotional development was in some way short-circuited in childhood. They grew up in homes where there was poor emotional modeling. As children, there was no balance between mind, will, and emotions. Their souls were undernourished; they were victims of emotional malnutrition. The cost is high. Not only do they endure unnecessary isolation, frustration, pain, and relational mediocrity, but without meaning to, they pass their dysfunctional legacy on to their children.

As Dwight and Julie began to understand the nature of emotions and the importance of balancing mind, will, and emotions, things began to fall into place for them. They realized that many of their problems stemmed from opposite, yet equally dysfunctional, attitudes about emotions.

Let's look at three types of people. The first two have under-developed parts of their personalities. They lack balance, have limited perception, and pockets of immaturity.

The Head-Over-Heart Person

The head-over-heart individuals place the greatest importance on the intellect, often ignoring the emotions. In time they become numb, and their feelings become frozen.

Recently, my wife and I rented the movie *Ordinary People*. It's the story of an upper-class suburban family. Everything is going well until they lose one of their sons in a drowning accident. Thrown into an emotional crisis, each family member responds differently. The mother copes by trying to ignore her emotions. She goes through each day with cold, detached, almost machinelike precision. She turns to perfectionism, control, and rigidity to anesthetize herself from facing the reality of the loss and feeling the range of emotions that come with healthy grief.

When our emotions become frozen, we miss the ambiance of life. Everything is black and white, and harmony turns to monotone. Uncomfortable with excitement and enthusiasm, we miss out on the highs and lows. We become critical, pessimistic, and lose our courage. We aren't even aware of our pain, so we're unable to express it. We wouldn't know how to clearly communicate our feelings anyway. We've been trained to articulate our ideas clearly but most of us had precious little training in clearly communicating our feelings. When we do try to express them, we come on too strong or not strong enough. We get embarrassed. People misunderstand. And we decide it's safer not to risk the humiliation of being rejected or laughed at, so we don't share.

David Mains put it like this:

> For a large part of my life I was tuned out emotionally. I wasn't aware of where others were coming from, and I didn't even understand my own feelings.

I was probably extreme in that regard. I didn't know when I was tired. I seldom paid attention to whether I was hot or cold. I wasn't in touch with what I liked or didn't like. If someone would ask me what was wrong, instead of saying, "I feel trapped with no way out of this situation," I'd reply, "I'm OK, why do you ask?"

Most of the time if someone accused me of expressing a negative emotion like anger or pride or frustration, I denied it. Was I stomping mad? No. Did I swear? Had my words stopped making sense because of my intense emotion? Never. What do you mean I was angry? You're accusing me of not acting the way a Christian should!

"You were emoting," my wife would tell me the next day. "It was as if you were sending out waves and waves of high voltage electricity. I don't understand how everybody can sense that except you."

Well, I wasn't in tune with my anger, my pain, my loneliness, my defensiveness, my fears, delights, moods, embarrassment, jealousies, whatever.

I functioned relatively well in the objective world of ideas and facts and words. But the more subjective realm of feeling was atrophying, shriveling up within me.

Thank God that in recent years the Lord has been doing a major healing in me for which I'm extremely grateful. One of the signs of health is that my feelings are coming back into play.[1]

Mains adds that when he reads the Bible now, he sees how much it has to say about emotions. When he goes to church, he often finds himself filled with inexplicable joy. He is able to shed tears when he is hurt, or when he discovers he has hurt someone else. And, he is better able to discern when he needs to rest.

The Heart-Over-Head Person

The second imbalance is as unhealthy as the first. These individuals are controlled by their emotions. They may have been raised by "head-over-heart" parents and have learned to mistrust their intellect. Their motto is "if you can't feel it, you can't trust it," or "if it's rational, it isn't relational."

While the head-over-heart individuals suffer from frozen

feelings, the heart-over-head individuals suffer from flooded feelings. While one deifies facts, the other deifies feelings. Feelings *are* facts to these people. If they feel it, it must be true. There's no need to ask questions or check it out. There's no possibility of misinterpretation—they interpret what you say by what they think you really mean.

Have you ever known someone like this? They are like emotional jellyfish, floating in and out with the tide. They are at the mercy of their emotions—blown here and there, often crashing against the rocks. They're difficult and draining to be around. When they say they've made up their minds, they really mean they've made up their emotions. They constantly feel misunderstood. When you try to reason with them, they see it as proof you don't understand them. If you catch them on a good day, okay; but catch them when they're down and watch out!

The problem with the heart-over-head individuals is that the emotions need the mind—and vice versa—to give balance. When our emotions are in control, the results can be disastrous.

In Scripture we find several examples of people who ignored their intellects and allowed their feelings to control them. For instance, we read that Saul's jealousy of David's popularity and success interfered with his ability to learn from his mistakes. Also, the Jews at Kadesh-Barnea allowed their anxiety to be in control, and it limited their ability to remember what God had already done for them. And, when Elijah allowed his depression to control him, he sat down under the juniper tree and asked to die.

The Head-and-Heart-in-Balance Person

By God's grace we have a third option. Before sin came into the world, our minds, wills, and emotions were in balance. Our Creator can bring them back into harmony with each other. God wants to help us recover from the effects of sin. He wants to restore the balance between our ability to think, choose, and feel. In fact, the process of sanctification is what heals our damaged emotions.

Applying Balance to Our Lives

In this chapter we've talked a lot about developing a healthy balance between mind, will, and emotions. Let's get specific now and begin looking at a general approach to dealing with the mind, will, and emotions.

How do the mind, will, and emotions function? How does what we think influence what we feel, and how does our thinking and feeling influence the choices we make? How can we grow in this area and help our children grow and achieve a balance between these three areas of their personalities?

BECOMING AWARE OF EMOTIONAL TRIGGERS

It's important for us to identify our feelings—which emotions do we experience frequently? Which are the most intense? Which ones last the longest? Our most frustrating question, though, may be determining why we have certain feelings. You see, emotions aren't rational—they don't always have a reason. Sometimes emotions just *are*. This is especially true when dealing with children's emotions. The most important question is not *why*, but *what* do you feel and *what* should we do about it?

Many of our emotional responses are triggered by incidental everyday events like being late for work because of heavy traffic, or having a flat tire on the expressway, or discovering just after cleaning the house that our kids have trashed the living room. But deeper emotional responses come from experiences in our past—experiences to which we have attached strong feelings. These experiences can come from a variety of sources. They can be caused by what happens to us, what we see happen to others, or in response to our own behavior. These events send signals to our brain. Our brain then processes and interprets the information based on similar past experiences. The emotion we attach to that experience depends upon our interpretation of that experience. In time, if we experience similar events, we will form emotional response habits that become subconscious and automatic.

EXAMINING OUR THOUGHTS AND ATTITUDES

While circumstances or events may strongly influence what we feel, they are rarely the sole cause of our emotions. The main cause of our emotions is not what happens to us, but how we choose to interpret it.

Dr. Archibald D. Hart has written that "feelings are often the end product of a series of irrational self-statements, and we can avoid prolonging the feeling or even triggering it in the first place by carefully examining the content of our thoughts, challenging their validity, and changing their content."[2]

Most specialists agree that children's thought processes hold the key to their feelings—that their misperceptions, misinterpretations, and irrational beliefs are at the core of emotional problems. For that reason, it's especially important when dealing with our children's emotions that we provide opportunities for them to test the accuracy of their perceptions about themselves and their world.

We can't change what happens to us, but we can change how we choose to interpret and respond to it. Our interpretations are the lenses through which we view reality—they color and clarify our world. If we interpret events in a positive way, we tend to have pleasant feelings. If we interpret them in a negative way, we have painful feelings. The problem is that many of us have inaccurate, irrational beliefs about life that cause us to misinterpret events in a negative way. These irrational beliefs produce a distorted perception of reality. Misconceptions children may have are:

- It's awful if others don't like me.
- I'm bad if I make a mistake.
- Everything should go my way; I should always get what I want.
- Things should come easy to me.
- The world should be fair and bad people must be punished.
- I shouldn't show my feelings.
- Adults should be perfect.
- There's only one right answer.
- I must win.
- I shouldn't have to wait for anything.[3]

The degree to which these or other irrational beliefs will lead to one or more emotional or behavioral problems in children depends in part on:

- the number of irrational beliefs the child holds;
- the range of situations in which the child applies his or her ideas (i.e., school, home, peers, adults, work, play);
- the strength of the child's belief, and
- the extent to which the child tends to distort reality as observed in errors of inference about what has happened or what will happen.[4]

TEACHING CHILDREN HEALTHY EMOTIONAL ATTITUDES

Children can be taught that their thoughts greatly influence what they feel. They can also learn that changing those thoughts can change how they feel. Kids can be taught to identify and give up irrational demandingness, to avoid tyrannical "shoulds," "musts," and "oughts," and to accept themselves as imperfect human beings who sometimes succeed, sometimes fail, and sometimes do stupid things. And they can learn that God will help them through it all.

Age has a lot to do with your child's ability to understand certain emotional concepts. Younger children (under seven years old) need to be given a language for identifying their feelings. We can teach them how to identify and express their emotions. We can teach them to replace negative, destructive self-talk with healthy, positive self-statements.

Older children can learn to evaluate their own thinking by more objective and rational criteria. They can evaluate self-talk in light of Scripture, learn from their parents, and from their own past experiences. They can also develop the ability to stand back and look at the bigger picture. And we can help them identify their own irrational beliefs when difficulties arise and learn healthier ways to interpret their situations.

As they learn to balance the different mental and emotional messages they receive from our minds and emotions, they'll be able to make better decisions.

TAKE ACTION

What traits and qualities do you want to characterize you and your children? Drs. Grace and Herbert Ketterman have listed twelve characteristics of emotional health. First, go through and circle the number that best represents your own current developmental level in each category. A "1" indicates no development in this area, a "5" indicates average development, and a "10" indicates excellent development. Next, go through and place your children's initials to indicate where each child is in his or her emotional development.

1. A loving adult who is capable of understanding and caring about himself and others:

    1   2   3   4   5   6   7   8   9   10

2. A careful adult who has learned how to achieve balances in her life—who values and appropriately expresses both her aggressiveness or anger and her vulnerability or fear—one who controls these without hiding or exploding them:

    1   2   3   4   5   6   7   8   9   10

3. A responsible adult who lives up to his own best, has an appropriate sense of duty, and is trustworthy:

    1   2   3   4   5   6   7   8   9   10

4. A cautious adult who shows good judgment by finding and considering most of the facts involved in making life's decisions (not just her own selfish viewpoint or wishes):

    1   2   3   4   5   6   7   8   9   10

5. A wise adult who knows how to learn from his own and others' experiences, and applies such learning to new situations:

    1   2   3   4   5   6   7   8   9   10

6. A creative adult who values her God-given talents and uses them for her own joy and the betterment of others:

    1   2   3   4   5   6   7   8   9   10

7. A courageous adult who will take appropriate risks but not those that needlessly hurt anyone:

    1   2   3   4   5   6   7   8   9   10

8. An adult who knows how to lose as well as how to win:

    1   2   3   4   5   6   7   8   9   10

9. An adventurous adult who explores more than he expects, but who expects the best of himself and others:

    1   2   3   4   5   6   7   8   9   10

10. A reverent adult who values life as a gift from God and who protects that life through proper care and knowledge:

    1   2   3   4   5   6   7   8   9   10

11. A flexible adult who can adapt to necessary changes when they are not damaging, but who holds to principles that dare not change:

    1   2   3   4   5   6   7   8   9   10

12. An achieving adult who is motivated to reach goals, but who will not sacrifice her integrity by taking advantage of others:

    1   2   3   4   5   6   7   8   9   10[5]

2

Growing Emotionally Healthy Children

Most parents have good intentions—they want to help their children become healthy, mature adults. But good intentions aren't enough. We need to create an environment that encourages growth.

ONE FATHER'S STORY

Paul shared a story with me that I've heard echoed again and again by frustrated parents.

It started out as a nice evening at home. He was downstairs working on the family's monthly finances while his eight-year-old daughter Natalie was upstairs practicing her piano exercises.

"In the past we've had struggles with her piano practicing because she refuses to count. What she played sounded great, so I decided to take a break to compliment her."

So far so good.

"After complimenting her, I asked, 'Will you play a couple of other pieces for me?'

"Suddenly, she lashed out in frustration, 'Nothing I ever do is good enough. I don't know why I even try!'

"Then, I became frustrated too. What I hoped would be an encouragement to Natalie became adversarial."

Put yourself in Paul's place.

- How would you feel?
- How would you have responded?
- What would you do next? Would you just stay in your office and ignore the incident until your child raises the subject, or would you begin a discussion?
- Does your child need to be disciplined?

As you work through this chapter, think about how Paul might have responded and what he should do next. At the end of the chapter, we'll discuss how Paul chose to respond to this situation.

SIX KEYS TO GROWING HEALTHY KIDS

1. Cultivate an encouraging environment.

What is an encouraging environment? It's a place where children feel valued—where parents spend more time building and encouraging them than scolding and correcting them, and where kids are honored and treated with respect. An encouraging environment is one where parents attempt to catch their children doing something right rather than wrong—where they invest more energy in praising them for being successful than criticizing them for falling short of their expectations.

A nurturing environment is one in which parents respond to their children's pleasant as well as painful emotions. Without intending to, many parents tend to respond more often to their children's out-of-control emotions. This teaches kids that the best way to get attention is to create a crisis.

A nurturing environment is one where it is safe to make mistakes. In fact, kids learn that it's not only safe, but that God can use their failures to help them grow. This lifestyle practices Romans 8:28. Kids learn to respond to mistakes by asking, "What can I learn from this experience?"

The best way to achieve this kind of environment is for

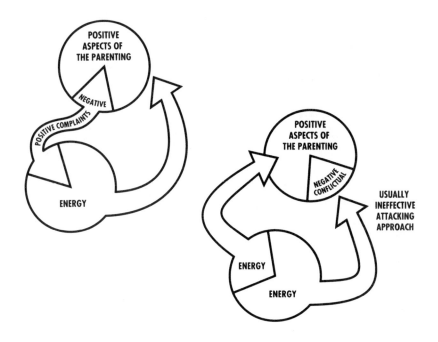

parents to model it. A couple I've been seeing for several months recently had an opportunity to practice this principle.

A Father's Example

I recently got this telephone call at my office. "Dr. Oliver, this is Judy Goertzen. I'm worried about Dick. I've never seen him so depressed. I know we have an appointment tomorrow afternoon, but I wonder if there's something I can do now to help him."

Dick had been raised in a family where men didn't express emotion. Real men were strong, self-sufficient, and stable. Anything that expressed weakness or need was a sign of spiritual immaturity, carnality, or a lack of faith. Dick remembered his dad saying, "Son, God has promised to supply all our needs, and if you're not happy, it must be because you aren't trusting God to be faithful to what He has promised."

It didn't take long for Dick to get the message.

Forty-two years of stuffing, repressing, suppressing, denying, and ignoring his feelings had created an emotional Mt. Saint Helens. With marital and financial difficulties escalating and pressures building, Dick's emotions had finally erupted.

Dick and Judy's adolescent children had noticed the dramatic change in their dad and were frightened by it. They had questioned Judy about what was wrong with him, but she didn't know what to tell them.

By the following day, Dick was doing better. He was still depressed, but the depression no longer controlled him. At the end of our session, I asked him, "Are you going to talk to your kids about what happened and why your behavior has been different this past week?"

"Are you serious?" he puzzled. "Why would I want to do that?"

In our previous sessions, we had talked about the legacy of being raised in a dysfunctional family. The impact on Dick was that he still felt like an emotional preadolescent. More than once he had stated that he didn't want to pass this legacy on to his kids.

"What better way to teach your children about emotions than to share with them what you are currently going through. What better way to practice Romans 8:28 than by letting them see it at work in your life," I urged.

"I just never would have thought of doing something like that," Dick replied. "What would I say to them?"

"You could talk about what happened to you," I explained. "You could discuss with them things like: What is depression? What are the symptoms? What causes it? And, how you are working through it and learning from it."

Judy jumped in, "What a great idea! We can teach them about emotions without lecturing them."

Together, we worked out a plan. Dick's experience became a turning point in that family's communication pattern. Because Dick had the courage to be honest with his kids and allowed them to work through his depression with him, the family received a valuable education on dealing with their emotions.

When Dick became more open and transparent, it became easier for his children to be open about their own concerns.

Dick and Judy discovered that both of their children had also struggled with depression. They had not been given permission to share it because of the unspoken rule in their home that said, "We don't have any emotional problems in this family."

Learning from our own mistakes is easier said than done. I recently found a faded photocopy of a letter from a father who realized he had blown it with his son that day. There was no name or date on it, and I have no idea where it came from. Yet, it illustrates the elements that go into cultivating an encouraging environment.

Father Forgets

Listen, son: I am saying this as you lie asleep, one little paw crumpled under your cheek and the blond curls stickily wet on your damp forehead. I have stolen into your room alone. Just a few minutes ago, as I sat reading my paper in the library, a stifling wave of remorse swept over me. Guiltily I came to your bedside. These are the things I was thinking, son: I had been cross to you. I scolded you as you were dressing for school because you gave your face merely a dab with a towel. I took you to task for not cleaning your shoes. I called out angrily when you threw some of your things on the floor.

At breakfast I found fault, too. You spilled things. You gulped down your food. You put your elbows on the table. You spread butter too thick on your bread. And as you started off to play and I made for my train, you turned and waved a hand and called, "Good-bye, Daddy!" and I frowned, and said in reply, "Hold your shoulders back!"

Then it began all over again in the late afternoon. As I came up the road I spied you, down on your knees, playing marbles. There were holes in your stockings. I humiliated you before your boyfriends by marching you ahead of me to the house. Stockings were expensive — and if you had to buy them you would be more careful! Imagine that, son, from a father!

Do you remember, later, when I was reading in the library, how you came in timidly, with a sort of hurt look in your eyes? When I glanced up over my paper, impatiently at the interruption, you hesitated at the door. "What is it you want?" I snapped. You said nothing, but ran across in one tempestuous plunge, and threw your arms around my neck and kissed me, and your small arms tightened with an affection that God has set blooming in your heart and which even neglect could not wither. And then you were gone, pattering up the stairs.

Well, son, it was shortly afterwards that my paper slipped from my hands and a terrible sickening fear came over me. What has habit been doing to me? The habit of finding fault, of reprimanding—this was my reward to you for being a boy. It was not that I did not love you; it was that I expected too much of youth. I was measuring you by the yardstick of my own years.

And there was so much that was good and fine and true in your character. The little heart of you was as big as the dawn itself over the wide hills. This was shown by your spontaneous impulse to rush in and kiss me good night. Nothing else matters tonight, son. I have come to your bedside in the darkness and I have knelt there, ashamed!

It is a feeble statement; I know you would not understand these things if I told them to you during your waking hours. But tomorrow I will be a real daddy! I will chum with you, and suffer when you suffer, and laugh when you laugh. I will bite my tongue when impatient words come. I will keep saying as if it were a ritual: "He is nothing but a boy—a little boy!"

I am afraid I have visualized you as a man. Yet as I see you now, son, crumpled and weary in your cot, I see that you are still a baby. Yesterday you were in your mother's arms, your head on her shoulder. I have asked too much, too much.[1]

2. Discover their unique design and start where they're at.

In the busyness of parenting, we can forget two things. The first is that our children are not adults, and that each child is unique. Without intending to, many parents lump all of their children together and forget that each child has unique needs because of differences in their personalities and developmental stages.

In Proverbs 22:6 we read, "Train up a child in the way he should go, even when he is old he will not depart from it" (NASB). For years Christians interpreted that verse to mean that parents decide the kind of person their child "should" be and then force the child into that mold. That's the cookie-cutter approach to parenting. But a closer look at this verse reveals that parents are being instructed to discover the God-given bent of each of their children and to adapt their training accordingly.

According to Chuck Swindoll, the most important aspect of parenting is knowing your child. In his book *You and Your Child,* he states, "The effectiveness of training your child is in direct proportion to the extent you know your child."[2]

He goes on to say, "In every child God places in our arms, there is a bent, a set of characteristics already established. The bent is fixed and determined before he is given over to our care. The child is not, in fact, a pliable piece of clay. He has been set; he has been bent. And the parent who wants to train this child correctly will discover that bent!"[3]

How can we discover the God-given design of our children? How are they individually unique? The first thing to understand is that the emotional development of children starts early. Although infants can't speak, their emotions are active. From the beginning, they experience warmth and cold, hunger and thirst, pleasure and pain, dampness and dryness, the comfort of being held and the discontent with not being held whenever they wish. They experience fright, anger, frustration, and desire.

Younger children may seem to be on an emotional roller coaster at times. One minute they're happy with excitement, and the next minute appear to be overcome with misery, pain, or frustration. At an early age, children are unable to interpret, influence, and deal with the painful or pleasurable stimulations of their environment.

3. Be available to your child.

This is the simplest of the six keys, but it is also the most difficult. It's simple because it doesn't involve reading or special training. Any living, breathing, and conscious human being can be available. Being available is difficult because we all have more to do than can be done in one day. By the end of each day, few of us feel we've accomplished all we set out to do. In the midst of this busyness, children can seem like an interruption.

Of course, it's unrealistic for us to always drop what we're doing to cater to the demands of our children, but, at the same time, we need to remember that kids don't have an adult sense of time. To them, the present is all there is. To kids, availability communicates our love. It's clearly the most important of the six keys as all the others depend on it.

There are two ways we can be available to them. First, we can set aside special time just for them each week. And we can take a few minutes with them each day when they wake in the morning, when they return from school, or before bedtime. As you study your children, you'll discover certain times during the day when they are more open to chatting. These moments are prime time for parents to dialogue with their kids about their day.

Timing can be so important. When possible pick a time that is unhurried for both you and your kids. If you hear yourself finishing a sentence for your child, or saying, "Yeah," "Uh-huh," "I get it," or "That's enough," you have most likely picked a bad time. A wise parent will set aside schedules as often as possible to read with their kids, play with them, or share their day.

Second, we can learn to "make" time when they need it, and to watch for teachable moments. In Luke 5:17-20 Christ was teaching a distinguished group of Pharisees and teachers of the law. They had come from miles to hear His message. In the middle of Christ's message, the tiles above His head began to move—well, they weren't just moving, they were removed. A paralyzed man was lowered on a stretcher directly in front of Jesus.

What a lousy time for an interruption. It probably ruined a really good presentation. Whether Jesus was making His second or third point or wrapping up a powerful closing, His flow must have been ruined. Yet, what most of us would view as an interruption, Jesus viewed as a unique opportunity. He saw the need, recognized their faith, and viewed it as more important than His lesson. He identified a teachable moment and took advantage of it.

We can learn to make time when meaningful opportunities arise. At times our children will want to talk immediately about the issues that concern them, at other times they'll need to think them through first—to process them. As parents, our role is to provide a safe place for them to process and communicate their concerns while working out solutions of their own.

Did you know that children spell love differently than adults do? Most children spell love with a *T*, an *I*, an *M*, and an *E*. That's right. *TIME* is how kids spell love. It's a myth that meaningful exchanges between parents and kids make up for a lack of time together. In *Key to Your Child's Heart*, Gary Smalley shares a powerful illustration of the importance of spending time with our children.

> A frightened eighteen-year-old boy standing in front of a stern judge listened as the judge, a close personal friend of the boy's father, told him that he was a disgrace to the community of his family: "You ought to be ashamed of yourself, disgracing your family's name, causing your parents a great deal of anguish and embarrassment. Your father is an upright citizen in this community. I have personally served on numerous committees with him and know of his commitment to his city. I count your father as a close personal friend and it is with deep grief that I have to sentence you this day for your crime."
>
> With his head bowed in obvious embarrassment, the young man listened to the judge. Then, before sentence was passed, he asked if he could speak: "Sir, I do not mean to be disrespectful or to make excuses for my behavior. But I envy you a great deal. You see, there were many days and nights that I wanted to be my father's best friend. There were many times when I needed his help with school work, in some of my dating situations, and in some of the difficult times that I faced as a teenager. But my father was gone a great deal, probably on some of these committees with you, or playing golf. I've always felt like other things were more important to him than I was. I don't mean this disrespectfully, but I truly wish I knew my father like you do."
>
> Stunned by the boy's words, the judge placed him on probation and ordered that the boy and his father were to spend time together every week, getting to know each other. The father obvi-

ously was humiliated by the sentence, realizing his lack of commitment to his son, but it caused him to get to know his son better and that was the turning point in his son's life.[4]

4. Look, listen, and then talk.

When it comes to good communication, most parents get the formula backward. We tend to talk, and talk, and talk, and then maybe look and listen. We usually place the greatest emphasis on the verbal elements of communication. You may be surprised to learn that words only account for 7 percent of a message. Tone of voice contributes 38 percent, and other nonverbal factors account for 55 percent. If we listen to just the words, we could miss up to 93 percent of the real meaning of what our children are trying to communicate.

When your kids are speaking, it's important to develop the habit of listening attentively to what they are saying. Notice I said "develop the habit." It's not easy or automatic to be a good listener. People tend to listen five times as fast as another person can speak. If your child speaks at 100 words per minute and you can listen at 500 words per minute, what do you do with your spare time? It's easy to become bored and daydream or mentally work on the next day's schedule. It requires deliberate effort and discipline to stay focused on being attentive.

You can show your interest in what your children are saying by smiling, nodding, using good eye contact, and allowing them to continue uninterrupted. Children often have more to say than parents have time for at the moment. When this happens, clearly communicate your interest in hearing more, explain why you must postpone your conversation until later, and promise to get back to the discussion as soon as possible. And then, make sure you keep your promise.

Effective listening requires more than merely hearing your kids' words. It means reading their nonverbal messages as well. They're reading yours. So, watch their facial expressions, their posture, their gestures, and ask yourself what each message communicates. It's especially easy to become impatient with children who are slow talkers. You may have a tendency to help these kids express themselves rather than listen beyond the words to what they really mean.

Tone of voice can teach us a lot about what our children are trying to tell us about themselves. We need to watch for differences in tone, tempo, texture, pace, and volume. Sometimes a change in tone of voice is due to emotional changes. At other times, it can reflect tiredness. But sometimes our children feel rushed to cram a lot of talk into a little time because they sense we're impatient with them. Learn to read your children's tone of voice, and then reflect back to them what you think they said. This lets them know how they're coming across and allows you to check the accuracy of your interpretation.

When you have developed good looking and listening skills, you will understand your children better. You will be better able to notice when something is going wrong.

Recently, I was able to use these skills in a situation with one of my sons.

"Matthew, how did your day go today?" I asked.

"Fine," he replied.

By his response I knew immediately that something was wrong. Why? Matthew rarely gives a one-word response to any kind of question. He is energetic, enthusiastic, and usually very positive. In fact, Matthew is a "live wire."

Because I had studied Matthew and understood his communication patterns, I was alerted to the fact that something might be wrong. Either he was tired, or he'd had a tough day, or was experiencing an emotion he didn't know how to express. When I checked out my suspicions, I discovered that something had happened at school. We were able to talk about it — well, I mostly listened and asked a few open questions. But, from that experience he learned something about his emotions, and I learned more about him.

5. When you do talk, ask questions.

The fifth key to raising emotionally healthy children is to learn the art of asking good questions. A question says, "I've been listening to you, I'm with you, you are worth taking the time to understand, your ideas and opinions are important to me, and you are important to me."

There are two kinds of questions: closed questions and open questions. A closed question is one that can be answered in one word, such as, "Did you have a nice day today?" An open-ended question is one that requires more than a one-word response, such as, "What was your favorite part of the day today?" It's usually better to ask several open-ended questions than several closed questions.

When asking a question, be sure to give your children enough time to respond. Often we ask questions we have thought about but our children haven't. If you ask a question, then push for a response too quickly, it can put pressure on your kids and send the wrong message. While we intend to communicate that our children are important, the message might be "What you have to say is important as long as you can say it quickly. I have a lot of other important things to do today."

When your children respond to your question, remember to listen carefully to what they say and how they say it. Both the content and the tone of their reply are important. If they respond in an enthusiastic and energetic way and if they volunteer even more information, you've hit on a key. Either you asked a great question, hit on a topic that's important to them, or found a time during the day that they are open to conversation.

6. *Give your children permission to express their emotions.*

Many of us have been taught to deny our true feelings. When we were depressed, we were told it was only discouragement. When we were sad, we were told to cheer up. When we were angry, we were told to keep our cool. When we felt pain, we were told to be brave and smile.

Dr. Haim G. Ginot has this to say about the importance of emotional development:

> Emotions are part of our genetic heritage. Fish swim, birds fly, and people feel. Sometimes we are happy, sometimes we are not; but sometimes in our life we are sure to feel anger and fear, sadness and joy, greed and guilt, lust and scorn, delight and disgust. While we are not free to choose the emotions that arise in us, we are free to choose how and when to express them, provided we know what they are.[5]

So, what's the solution? Emotional education. It's actually more important for children to know what they feel than why they feel it—they are less likely to feel "all mixed up" inside.

If our children are going to have a solid foundation for their later emotional life, they need to be encouraged to both experience and express a wide range of emotions. Their emotional experience must not be limited to pleasant emotions. If they are only allowed to experience one side of their emotions, they will have a limited awareness of who they are and a distorted perspective of others. They will be severely limited in their ability to learn important emotional lessons and they will be more vulnerable to being controlled by their emotions.

Children should not only be allowed, but enthusiastically encouraged to experience happiness and sadness, hope and fear, joy and depression, jealousy and compassion.

Dr. Thomas Armstrong, author of *In Your Own Way,* believes that proper emotional expression is so important to childhood development that real learning can't take place in the absence of both pleasant and painful emotions. He states that:

> To ignore this complex web of feelings is not simply unwise—it is impossible. Yet this is often what we try to do when helping youngsters at home or school. We attempt to deny their emotional lives and, in so doing, cut them off from the source of energy that connects them to their own natural powers of learning.
>
> Children need to have permission to express their joy and anger freely while learning so that the vitality locked up in these emotions can be transformed into the mental activities associated with academic progress. This doesn't mean that you need to let your kids run roughshod over your life, doing whatever they want. It does require, however, that your child's honest expression of emotion in all of its colors be acknowledged, and that your child be given opportunities for channeling his true feelings in a number of positive directions.[6]

There is growing neuropsychological evidence supporting the central role emotions have in learning. Dr. Thomas Armstrong writes about the significant relationship between feeling and thinking in the learning process.

> We tend to think of learning—at least academic learning—as a mental process. Yet recent evidence from the brain sciences suggests that the emotions are vital to higher abstract thinking processes.

He concludes that:

> It's really this balance between feeling and thinking that's most important in the education of the child. . . . Emotionally flat classrooms fail to teach because they neglect the emotional brain.[7]

Medical research has shown that there are three distinct parts of the human brain. The reptilian brain controls some of our deepest and most instinctive behaviors—territoriality and assertiveness rituals such as prancing, preening, and posturing. It tends to express itself most directly in the actions of mobs and gangs.

The rational brain consists of the two hemispheres referred to as the neocortex. This part of the brain is the source of our highest abstract thinking processes, including the symbolic functions necessary for reading, writing, and arithmetic.

The limbic system is our emotional brain. It controls many of our emotional responses to the environment, including rage, fear, grief, and joy. The limbic system is located in the center of the brain. Researchers believe that it functions as a crossroads for much of what goes on within the central nervous system, uniting emotional impulses in the lower brain with rational thought patterns in the higher brain.

Dr. Paul Maclean has written that "The only part of the brain that can tell us what we perceive to be real things is the limbic brain."[8]

Dr. William Gray has added that "Ideas are rooted in emotional codes." He calls these codes "feeling-tones."[9] He says that these emotional tones are embedded in neuropsychological processes and serve as vehicles through which rational ideas are remembered, associated, and reported.

In terms of our children, he is saying that kids will often get more out of the *way* something is taught than from what is being taught. Sometimes the emotional tone of the classroom has greater impact than the specific content of the curriculum.

If information is taught to our children with anger, enthusiasm, lethargy, or sadness, how it was taught may stand out much more in children's minds than the specific facts or ideas contained in the lesson.

Think back to your own childhood. Which memories of your mother or father stand out in your mind? For most of us, they are the experiences that involved strong emotion. The times we were disciplined out of anger are probably the most vivid.

Watch your children. Look for the emotions that might be registered on their faces. Take stock of the emotional stresses affecting them. Whenever possible, encourage them to talk about any and all of their worries and feelings. Encourage them to share whatever they are feeling — positive or negative, pleasant or painful. If it's hard for them to open up, you can "prime the pump" by sharing some of your own feelings.

Invite your children to interact with you. Encourage them to elaborate on what they are saying. Ask questions like:

"Would you like to help?"

"I'd like to hear about how your day went."

"Tell me more about that."

"Then what happened?"

"You look upset. If you'd like to talk about it, I'd like to listen."

Also helpful are simple phrases that help a child better understand what he or she is communicating, such as:

"You look like you are really angry."

"It sounds like your feelings are hurt."

"It seems like you are afraid that you won't do well on the test."

Please remember too that it's easy for parents to only notice and talk about problem emotions. If that's all we focus on, our kids will learn that those are the only ones worth expressing. Take time to notice all of their emotions.

PAUL'S SOLUTION

Remember the story of Paul and his daughter Natalie? Well, here's how he chose to respond.

"I decided to go upstairs to talk with her. I said, 'Natalie, I'd like to talk with you for a few minutes. Would you be willing to talk to me?' Almost before I got the words out of my mouth, she said, 'Sure, Dad.' I sat down on the end of her bed, and we began to chat.

"As we talked, it came out that the primary issue wasn't how I was trying to help her, but that she wanted to rush through her lesson so she could watch a favorite television program. When I sat down to help her, it looked like she would miss her show.

"We were able to discuss what happened and different ways she could have responded. In that conversation, both of us expressed a wide range of emotions."

Listen carefully when your kids talk. What is their level of emotional understanding? What do they see as their options? What other factors might be influencing their emotional responses? For example, as Natalie and Paul talked, Paul found out that Natalie was concerned about some minor problems at school. While unrelated to the piano incident, it opened a whole new area for them to discuss.

TAKE ACTION

Several years ago I saw an advertisement for a course that could help students get better grades. Several television celebrities were interviewed and shared how it helped their children significantly increase their school performance. As I read through the parents' manual, I found a tool that is helpful for evaluating my performance as a parent.

So, take the test and grade yourself. Just remember, don't be too hard on yourself; with a little "homework" you can always bring up your grade.

Report Card for Parents

A B C D F   1. Do I praise my child at least once a day?
A B C D F   2. Do I treat my child as a worthwhile member of our family?

A B C D F   3. Am I available when my child wishes to talk to me?

A B C D F   4. Do I include my child in family plans and decisions?

A B C D F   5. Do I set reasonable guidelines and insist that my child follow them?

A B C D F   6. Do I treat my child the way I treat my best friends?

A B C D F   7. Do I treat my children equally?

A B C D F   8. If I tell my children to do something, do I frequently take the time to help them understand why instead of saying: "because I said so"?

A B C D F   9. Do I set a good example for my child?

A B C D F 10. Do I think positive thoughts about my child and encourage achievements?

A B C D F 11. Do I take an interest in my child's education and attend PTA meetings?

A B C D F 12. Do I occasionally give my child a hug or friendly pat on the back?

A B C D F 13. Do I encourage attendance at weekly religious services?

A B C D F 14. Do I spend time each day looking over my children's schoolwork with them?

A B C D F 15. Do I send my child off to school each day with a kind word of encouragement?

A B C D F 16. Does my child see me pray?

A B C D F 17. Does my child see me reading the Bible?

A B C D F 18. Does my child hear me apologize when I am wrong?

A B C D F 19. Do I talk to my child about my emotions?[10]

Parenting by Design

If I do not want what you want, please try not to tell me that my want is wrong.

Or if I believe other than you, at least pause before you correct my view.

Or if my emotion is less than yours, or more, given the same circumstances, try not to ask me to feel more strongly or weakly.

Or yet if I act, or fail to act, in the manner of your design for action, let me be. I do not, for the moment at least, ask you to understand me. That will come only when you are willing to give up changing me into a copy of you. I may be your spouse, your parent, your offspring, your friend, or your colleague. If you will allow me any of my own wants, or emotions, or beliefs, or actions, then you open yourself, so that some day these ways of mine might not seem so wrong, and might finally appear to you as right — for me.

To put up with me is the first step to understanding me. Not that you embrace my ways as right for you, but that you are no longer irritated or disappointed with me for my seeming waywardness. And in understanding me you might come to prize my differences from you, and, far from seeking to change me, preserve and even nurture those differences.[1]

In the mid-'70s I moved from Southern California to Central Nebraska. With only a few pieces of furniture, the big old farmhouse I rented seemed bare. A friend suggested I fill the place with plants—they enrich the air, add warmth and character, are attractive, and cheaper than furniture. It sounded like a good idea.

I selected about ten different plants from a nearby nursery. As I chose each plant, the clerk explained to me its unique needs—like when to prune and fertilize it, how much water and light it required, and whether it was fragile or hearty.

Unfortunately for the plants, I ignored the clerk's advice—after all, a plant is a plant. . . . Right?

Wrong!

My philosophy on plant care went something like this: if a little of something is good, a lot is better. I placed three fertilizer spikes in each pot instead of the one recommended, watered them generously and often, and even hauled them outside on weekends to bathe in the sunshine. I was sure to be rewarded with new buds of growth.

Within three weeks, they had all died. I felt betrayed. I'd given those plants everything I thought they needed—in fact, I gave them a lot of what I thought they needed. I had faithfully nourished them . . . or so I thought. Where did I go wrong?

Returning to the nursery, I told the clerk what I'd done. She laughed. I didn't—those plants were expensive. She explained to me that my mistake was to treat all the plants as if they were the same. I hadn't given them what they needed. Instead, I gave them what I thought they needed.

"Each plant is different," she explained. "What may nourish one will kill another. It's important to learn the unique needs of each species and treat them accordingly."

I bought new plants that day, but this time I wrote down everything the clerk told me about each one. I followed her instructions to the letter, and guess what? My plants flourished. They blossomed and sprouted new growth.

Many parents approach parenting like my first attempt at indoor horticulture. They think they know their children's needs without first understanding their individual uniqueness.

UNDERSTANDING THE NEEDS OF YOUR CHILDREN

We often think we can nourish our children the way we would like to be nourished. In fact, we give them generous doses of the things we think they need, assuming that what nourishes us will nurture them too. It doesn't work, and we become frustrated, disappointed, and discouraged.

The problem is that the process of nurturing involves looking, listening, and studying those special little people. It means taking the time to find out what they need and want, learning their language, and discovering how to love them in ways that are meaningful to them. What communicates love to us may be quite different from what says "I love you" to our kids.

Reading Your Kids' Nonverbal Language

Your children will tell you much about themselves through what they do, as well as what they say. Their nonverbal communication contains a wealth of information for parents who have learned to listen with their eyes as well as with their ears. I learned this many years ago when our retarded son Matthew lived at home. He couldn't communicate his needs to us verbally. He would grasp our hands and place them on his head or rub his head against us to show us that something was wrong. We learned to read his body movements and his eyes to detect any type of seizure activity. In time, I found that I had also begun to listen to my clients with my eyes and hear what they could not put into words.

What do your kids' facial expressions tell you? Sometimes we attempt to cover up our facial expression so they don't give away our thoughts and feelings. For example, we may use our hands to cover our mouth when we tell a lie. Children, adolescents, and adults have their own variation of covering lies. Kids usually use one or both hands to cover their mouths right after they tell a lie. A teenager may bring a hand to his mouth, but instead of covering his mouth, he rubs his lips lightly with a finger. Adults usually raise their hand to cover their mouth, but tend to touch the bottom part of their nose instead. Think about it and watch. Use this information cautiously. For instance, I wouldn't suggest you go around accusing others of lying based on this test!

Sometimes we scratch our heads when we are puzzled or touch our noses when we are in doubt. Often when a person wants to interrupt, he tugs on one ear. Frustration or anger is displayed when someone rubs his or her neck. What does your children's nonverbal language tell you? What are they saying to you when they clench their hands, cross their arms, put their hands on their hips, put their hands behind their back, or put them in their pockets? Hands on the hips can convey impatience. Hands behind the back may mean that person is not currently feeling in control. Crossing the arms can indicate defensiveness. When your children begin supporting their head with a hand during a class or in church, watch out for boredom—it's sneaking up on them.

Recognizing Your Children's Learning Styles

In addition to their nonverbals, it's important to remember that your kids perceive life through three avenues: what they see, what they hear, and what they feel. But in each of us, one perceiving apparatus—either seeing, hearing, or feeling—is more dominant than the others. Your children's dominant channel for perceiving life is the root of their learning style. Those children who are seeing-oriented learn best with their eyes (visual aids, diagrams, reading, pictures, video presentations, etc.). I am a seeing-oriented person. Things just register better with me when I can see them. That's why I prefer speaking to groups of people in person rather than on the radio. It helps me when I can see my audience and read their nonverbal communication.

Those children who are hearing-oriented learn best with their ears (lectures, audio tapes, oral instructions, listening, etc.). And those children who are feeling-oriented learn best through intuitive perception (spiritual insight, inner sense, emotional impact, etc.).

If you have a hard time communicating with your child, it may be because you are not appealing to his or her dominant channel of perception and learning style. If you repeatedly tell your child to put his dirty clothes in the hamper and can't understand why he persists in throwing them in his closet after so many verbal warnings, you may not be speaking his language. It's as if the child is deaf, and in a sense, he may be. He may be seeing-oriented or feeling-oriented. Your verbal lectures and warnings don't get through to him as readily. Because of that, you may not be speaking to him in the language he understands best.

In order to communicate effectively, you may need to translate your message into your child's language. If you don't know your child's learning style, try communicating in all three styles and notice which one provokes the best response. As an example, if your child does not respond to your verbal instructions to put his dirty clothes in the hamper, try appealing to his visual sense. Tape a simple, colorful, handmade poster to his bedroom door or bathroom mirror showing a hand dropping a dirty shirt into the hamper.

Perhaps you could appeal to his feelings. Talk to him about the sense of accomplishment he will enjoy after several successful days of putting his dirty clothes in the hamper. Tell him how good you feel when he responds to your instructions. Talk about the importance of pleasing God with obedience. Put smiley face stickers on the hamper or on his napkin at the dinner table when he succeeds.

With a little time and ingenuity, you can discover the perceiving/learning style of each of your children. Listen to their terminology. The words they use may give you a clue. Children who say things like "I see what you mean," or "Let me see it, Mommy," may be seeing-oriented. Children who make comments like, "Tell me again, Daddy," or "I hear what you're saying," may be hearing-oriented. And children who say, "That story makes me happy," or "I feel bad when I disobey," may be feeling-oriented.

Your Kids' Eyes Can Tell You a Lot

Let's put this together with your children's nonverbals. The eye movements of children are not random movements. They have a specific purpose. Perhaps there are times when you wonder if, by their lack of eye contact, your kids are uncomfortable, daydreaming, or simply not listening. But other things may be possible. Watching your kids' eyes as you converse with them will give you a clue to what they are thinking. Does that sound like mind reading? Before you dismiss this idea, read on. Listening with your eyes is an undeveloped skill for most parents. But the information will make you a better listener with your children.

Eye movements are a doorway to your children's thoughts. For example, if they shift their eyes up and to the right, they are in the process of constructing a visual image.

If your kids shift their eyes up and to the left, they are recalling some previous images.

If your children keep their eyes level and to the right, they are in the process of constructing sounds.

If your kids keep their eyes level and shift them to the left, they are remembering previously heard sounds.

If your children look down and to the right, they are experiencing feelings.

If your kids are looking down and to the left, they are probably talking to themselves.

Many left-handed individuals will be reversed with respect to this chart.

In your conversations with your children, the proper use of questions can encourage them to share what they are experiencing as well as convey to them your sensitivity to their feelings and circumstances. Too often we use general questions such as, "What are you thinking?" or, "What are you feeling?" which may miss the mark. If your children shift their eyes up and to the right, how would you respond? You might say, "I wonder what picture is coming to your mind at this time?" or, "I wonder what it looks like to you?"

If they look up and to the left, you could say, "I wonder what picture from your photo album is coming to your mind right now?" If they look to the right, but their eyes are level, you could say, "Perhaps you're beginning to hear how this sounds."

If your kids are looking level and to the left, a question like, "How did that sound to you when you first heard it expressed?" would be appropriate. Or, "Do you remember hearing her make that statement to you?"

As they look down and to the right, you might respond with, "It appears you might be feeling something at this time," or "I would like to catch the feeling you're experiencing at this time," or "You appear to be sensing something at this moment."

As they look down and to the left, you could respond, "If I could listen into your mind right now, I would wonder what you're saying." Different? Yes! But it's another way of listening to your kids.[2]

UNDERSTANDING THE DIFFERENCES

If you've ever observed families with more than one child, you've probably at some point been amazed by the fact that children from the same gene pool, raised by the same parents, in the same neighborhood, eating the same diet, and going to the same school and church can be totally different.

What accounts for these differences?

- Why do some children love to sit and play alone for hours on end and others go crazy if other children aren't around?
- Why is one child always coming up with new ideas and inventing things while another child is content to play with toys the way he's "supposed to"?
- Why do some children like to talk things out while others prefer to work it all out inside and then talk about it?
- Why does one child welcome a new baby-sitter and another act as if it's the end of the world?

- How can some children read a book for an hour without being bored or distracted while others start climbing the wall after only minutes?
- Why do some children take pride in having a clean and neat room while other kids' rooms appear as if they had been used for nuclear testing?

APPRECIATING THE DIFFERENCES

In Psalm 139:14 we read King David's words, "I will give thanks to Thee, for I am fearfully and wonderfully made; Wonderful are Thy works" (NASB). Christians believe that every person is made in the image of God and is of infinite worth and value. We acknowledge that every person is unique. Yet, as parents most of us find it much easier to value the traits we see in our children that are similar to ours. I've heard parents make comments like, "Tommy is just like me, but I'm not sure where Jill came from. She is so different from the rest of us."

We've already discussed the importance of understanding God's unique design for each of our children. We saw that Proverbs 22:6 encourages us to discover the unique traits of our children's personalities and to raise them accordingly. We are exhorted to approach each child differently because each one is divinely different.

But how can we understand and make sense of the differences? First, we need to appreciate individual differences. In 1 Corinthians 12:14, we learn that diversity does not necessitate division. We can learn to maximize our differences. And second, it helps if we can make sense of those differences.

One of the most helpful tools for understanding and appreciating natural personality differences in people was developed by Swiss psychiatrist Carl Jung. In 1921, he suggested that many of what on the surface appears to be random variations in human behavior, are actually quite orderly and consistent. After years of observation, he found that some of the most important personality traits can be grouped into three basic patterns. He suggested that people can be more easily understood when we know how they prefer to take in information, the kind of information that is important to them, how they process that information to make decisions, and where they tend to focus their attention.

Psychological or personality type provides a kind of map to understanding people. Keep in mind that, while a map doesn't give us all the information we need, it does point us in the right direction.

Personality type consists of broad inborn preferences or tendencies that have a strong impact on individual differences. Everyone begins life with a few inherited traits that are the fundamental building blocks of his or her personality. These core traits interact with environmental influences in developing the personality as a whole. Every child has the capacity to function as an initiator, a reinforcer, and a responder:

Initiator: one who creates his own environment.

Reinforcer: one who selectively rewards or punishes people in his environment.

Responder: one who modifies the impact of the environment on his personality.[3]

THE MYERS-BRIGGS TYPE INDICATOR

Several years after Jung's basic findings were published, a mother and daughter team in the United States significantly expanded his foundational work. Based on years of careful research and observation, Isabel Briggs Myers and her mother Katherine Briggs added a fourth category and began to develop a useful tool to help measure these dimensions. The end result is known today as the Myers-Briggs Type Indicator (MBTI).

The MBTI identifies four sets of contrasting personality traits: extrovert and introvert, sensor and intuitive, thinker and feeler, judger and perceiver. Each trait can be identified by its complete name or by the single letter assigned to it.

Extroversion (E) _____ Focus Attitude _____ (I) Introversion
Sensing (S) _____ Perceiving Function _____ (N) Intuition
Thinking (T) _____ Deciding Function _____ (F) Feeling
Judging (J) _____ Lifestyle Attitude _____ (P) Perception

According to the "type" theory, everyone uses all eight of the traits, but one out of each of the four pairs is preferred and better developed. It's similar to the fact that, while we have two hands and use both of them, we tend to prefer one hand over the other. Most people are either right-handed or left-handed. When using your most preferred hand, tasks are usually easier, take less time, are less frustrating, and the end result is usually better.

To illustrate the significance of this point, try this exercise. On a piece of paper write your name with your right hand. Now write it with your left. One of the first things you'll notice is how awkward it feels when using your less-preferred hand. The results can be frustrating, inefficient, time-consuming, and inferior.

That's the way it is with personality type. When we are forced to face certain life tasks with one of our less-preferred and less-developed traits, the activity feels awkward, frustrating, takes more time and concentration, and often produces an inferior result.

When you put together the possible combinations on each one of the four levels, you end up with 16 different personality types. Each type is represented by four letters. The first letter is either E or I. The second letter is either S or N. The third letter is either T or F. The fourth letter is either J or P.

Before going on to explain the basic categories and looking at how they apply to your children, it would be helpful for you to take a short quiz to determine your own preferences.

TAKE ACTION

Word Choice Quiz
Taken from *One of a Kind* by LaVonne Neff

Here are 36 word pairs. In most cases, one word of each pair will seem more like your style than the other one.

Number a sheet of paper from 1 to 36. (It will be easier to find your score if you make two columns, just as the word pairs are given.) Write down the letter of the word you prefer in each pair.

As soon as they take the MBTI or some other personality type indicator, most people look immediately for a description of their own type. Then as soon as they've digested it, they try to locate their spouse, their children, their impossible boss, their friends.

You can do that too. At the end of the chapter, you'll find a short description of each of the 16 types.

Does your description fit you? If so, write your four letters in the front of this book so you won't forget them. If not, read other descriptions until you find one that sounds more like you.

1. a. people
    b. places

2. a. structure
    b. freedom

3. a. forest
    b. trees

4. a. mercy
    b. justice

5. a. reflect
    b. act

6. a. organized
    b. flexible

7. a. broad
    b. deep

8. a. curious
    b. decisive

9. a. facts
    b. possibilities

10. a. head
    b. heart

11. a. observant
    b. imaginative

12. a. enthusiastic
    b. consistent

13. a. party
    b. library

14. a. plan
    b. improvise

15. a. theoretical
    b. practical

16. a. question
    b. answer

17. a. private
    b. public

18. a. work
    b. play

19. a. write b. speak	20. a. cool b. warm
21. a. city b. forest	22. a. manager b. entrepreneur
23. a. contented b. restless	24. a. truth b. tact
25 a. production b. design	26. a. order b. harmony
27. a. look b. leap	28. a. values b. logic
29. a. insightful b. sensible	30. a. fair b. kind
31. a. change b. conserve	32. a. start b. finish
33. a. tortoise b. hare	34. a. relational b. analytical
35. a. discuss b. consider	36. a. process b. outcome

Key

1. After each number, circle the letter of the answer you chose.
2. For each vertical column (E, I, S, etc.), count the number of circled letters and write the total in the space provided below.
3. Notice that the vertical columns are arranged in four groups of two: E/I, S/N, T/F, and J/P. Take the letter with the highest total in each group, and write it at the bottom of the chart ("My Personality Type Code"). For example, if you circled 3 E-answers and 6 I-answers, write I in the first space.

4. To understand what your four-letter code means, keep reading this chapter!

	E	I	S	N			T	F	J	P
1.	a	b				2.			a	b
3.			b	a		4.	b	a		
5.	b	a				6.			a	b
7.	a	b				8.			b	a
9.			a	b		10.	a	b		
11.			a	b		12.	b	a		
13.	a	b				14.			a	b
15.			b	a		16.			b	a
17.	b	a				18.			a	b
19.	b	a				20.	a	b		
21.	a	b				22.			a	b
23.			a	b		24.	a	b		
25.			a	b		26.	a	b		
27.	b	a				28.	b	a		
29.			b	a		30.	a	b		
31.			b	a		32.			b	a
33.			a	b		34.	b	a		
35.	a	b				36.			b	a

TOTALS
(E:____ I:____) (S:____ N:____). (T:____ F:____) (J:____ P:____)

My Probable Personality Type Code: ____ ____ ____ ____
(E/I) (S/N) (T/F) J/P)[4]

DEFINING TYPES

Now that you have some general insights on the nature of personality and an idea of what your preferences are, let's get more specific. Here's a brief overview of the eight individual traits that make up the four categories. Let's look at them through the lives of eight different children. You'll probably see some of your own children, and maybe even yourselves, in these illustrations.

1. Sensing/Intuition

At any given time we are either taking in information or making decisions based upon information we have already received. Sensing and Intuition are two different ways of perceiving or gathering information.

Those who prefer the sensing (S) function are influenced more by what they actually see, hear, touch, taste, and smell than by the possibilities of what might be. They are not necessarily more sensible or sensitive. Karen is a sensor. While she uses her intuitive function, she prefers or is better at sensing. She has a here-and-now orientation. She is very observant and pays attention to detail; she stays focused on the task at hand and prefers to deal with things that are practical. When she colors, she likes to stay within the lines.

The intuition (N) function processes information by way of a sixth sense or hunch. Scott prefers intuition. While he uses his sensing function, he prefers or is better at intuition. He has more of a future orientation. Sometimes in school he finds it hard to concentrate on what the teacher is saying because he is thinking about the possibilities and options of a previous statement. He can get bored with details or mundane tasks. He loves to create. When he colors, he isn't too concerned about staying within the lines. He looks at what is and imagines what might be. When Karen is asked a question, she gives a specific answer. When Scott is asked a question, he usually gives a more general answer and tends to answer several other questions at the same time.

Sensing	Intuitive
Looks at specific parts and pieces.	Looks at patterns and relationships.
Lives in the present, enjoying what's there.	Lives toward the future, anticipating what might be.
Prefers handling practical matters.	Prefers imagining possibilities and exploring options.
Likes things that are definite and measurable.	Likes opportunities for being creative.

Starts at the beginning and takes one step at a time.	Jumps in anywhere and leaps over steps.
Enjoys reading instructions and notices details.	Skips instructions and follows hunches.
Likes set procedures, and clearly established routine.	Likes change and variety.
May seem too practical and literal-minded to Ns.	May seem fickle, impractical, and like a dreamer to Ss.[5]

2. Thinking/Feeling

Thinking (T) and Feeling (F) are two different ways of making decisions. Whenever we make decisions, we utilize both the thinking and feeling functions, but we prefer and are better at one or the other. Those who prefer the thinking function tend to decide on the basis of linear logic and objective considerations. The feeling function decides more on the basis of relational logic and personal subjective values.

Tim is a nine-year-old who, when making decisions, prefers the thinking function. When Tim is asked to do something, he is likely to ask "why?" It's not that he's being rebellious or unemotional, he simply prefers to make decisions based on reasons. Tim wants to know "why" and "just because" is not an acceptable answer for him.

At times Tim wonders why his sister seems to be so emotional. If someone disagrees with him, he is likely to want to know his or her reasons. Honesty and fairness are very important to him. He tends to see things as either black or white, right or wrong. Sometimes Tim can be so matter-of-fact that he comes across as cold and uncaring. But that's not true. Tim is a tender and sensitive little boy.

Karen's preferred decision-making function is feeling. Her decision-making process is more person-centered or value-oriented. That doesn't mean she is more emotional or illogical, though. While Tim tends to approach problems in an objective manner, Karen's preferred approach is more subjective.

Karen thinks as well as Tim does, but as a feeling-preferred type, she simply incorporates different values into the decision-making process. If someone disagrees with Karen, she will often let it go because she wants to maintain harmony and not make waves.

When it comes to making a decision, Karen will weigh heavily the feelings of others. It is easy for her to put herself in someone else's shoes. She is concerned about how her actions affect others. At times she is so concerned about others that she forgets to take care of her own needs. Because of her desire to please, Karen is likely to unquestioningly do what people ask of her. Feeling children can be especially sensitive to the emotional climate of their home. Constant conflict can cause them emotional, and even physical problems.

Thinking	Feeling
Decides with the head.	Decides with the heart.
Goes by linear logic and the bottom line.	Goes by relational logic and personal convictions.
Concerned with truth and justice.	Concerned with relationships and harmony.
Sees things as an onlooker, from outside a situation.	Sees things as a participant, from inside a situation.
Takes a long view.	Takes an immediate and personal view.
Spontaneously finds flaws and criticizes.	Spontaneously finds strength and appreciates.
Good at analyzing plans.	Good at understanding people.
May seem cold and condescending to Fs.	May seem fuzzy-minded and emotional to Ts.[6]

3. Extroversion/Introversion

Extroversion (E) and Introversion (I) are two different ways of relating to the outer world. They identify where we are most comfortable focusing our attention and what energizes us. Everyone uses extroversion and introversion but prefers, and is more comfortable with one of them.

An extrovert's primary source of energy is from the environment, the outer world of people and things. They are generally more comfortable when they are focusing on the people and activities around them.

Kelsey prefers extroversion. She has an outgoing and bubbly personality. She has a lot of friends at school and prefers playing with several friends to being alone. She is stimulated by interacting with people. She is at ease with strangers and comfortable with the world around her. She processes information by talking about it. When Kelsey comes home from school, she immediately wants her friends to come over.

An introvert's primary source of energy is from within, the inner world of reflection. They are energized by having time alone. They aren't necessarily quiet and unsociable, but they tend to be more comfortable focusing on the inner world of thoughts and ideas.

While Kelsey has a difficult time being alone, John loves to spend time by himself reading, thinking, or building something new with his Legos. He is energized by being alone. John is friendly and likes people, but he doesn't seek out large groups. He has a couple of best friends, and that's enough for him. When John comes home from school, he will often go to his room or to his fort in the backyard to read or work on a project. He tends to say little until he has known a person for awhile. When you ask Kelsey a question, she will respond immediately. In fact, she may respond before you finish your question. When you ask John a question, he prefers to have time to think about it before answering.

Extroversion	Introversion
Believe that the *unlived* life in not worth examining.	Believe that the *unexamined* life is not worth living.

Energized by other people and external experiences.	Energized by inner resources and experiences.
Acts and then (maybe) reflects.	Reflects and then (maybe) acts.
Is often friendly, talkative, and easy to know.	Is often reserved, quiet, and hard to know.
Expresses emotions.	Keeps emotions to themselves.
Needs relationships.	Needs privacy.
Thinks during or after speaking.	Thinks before speaking.
Gives breadth to life.	Gives depth to life.
May seem shallow to I's.	May seem withdrawn to E's.[7]

4. Judging/Perception

Judging (J) and Perception (P) are known as the lifestyle attitudes. These are the two opposites that were added by Meyers and Briggs. They reflect two different lifestyle orientations and two different ways people relate to the outside world.

A judging lifestyle is decisive, planned, and orderly. Kyle prefers a judging lifestyle, but that doesn't mean he is a judgmental person. He relates to the external world in a structured and organized way. Even as a little baby, Kyle loved to line up his toys in a straight line. He had a certain place for everything, and he would get upset if things weren't where they should be. While he can be spontaneous, he prefers order and structure. He enjoys knowing what the schedule is and keeping to it. He doesn't want to be late for his Sunday School class. Too much change throws him off.

Those who prefer a perceptive lifestyle tend to be more

flexible, adaptable, and spontaneous. Ps aren't necessarily more perceptive than Js; however, they are more curious and flexible, and handle changes better. Megan relates to the outer world in a very casual and laid-back manner. She could care less if things are in a straight line or if they are scattered all over the floor. She enjoys surprises and responds well to the unexpected. Megan is easily distracted. She starts projects and often has difficulty completing them because something else catches her attention. She is a lot of fun and brings fun and laughter to those around her.

Judging	Perceptive
Prefers an organized life-style.	Prefers a flexible and spontaneous lifestyle.
Likes definite order and structure.	Likes going with the flow.
Likes to have life under control.	Prefers to experience life as it happens.
Enjoys making decisions.	Enjoys getting more information.
Likes clear limits and categories.	Likes freedom to explore without limits.
Feels comfortable establishing closure.	Feels comfortable maintaining openness.
Enjoys deadlines and likes to plan in advance.	Meets deadlines by last-minute rush.
The product is more important than the process.	The process is more important than the product.
The most important part of a trip is arriving at the destination.	The most important part of the trip is traveling to a destination.

May seem demanding, rigid, and uptight to Ps.	May seem disorganized, messy, and irresponsible to Js.[8]

What are some of the benefits of understanding your child's S/N, T/F, E/I, and J/P preferences? What are some possible consequences for not understanding your child's preferences?

Go back over each of the descriptive lists and imagine what it would be like to have one preference, but to be raised in a home where you were expected to be the total opposite. Imagine what it would be like to be a feeling child who was talked to and expected to act like a thinker. What would be the message? Would there tend to be more miscommunication and conflict? Would you tend to feel misunderstood and out-of-place? Would you be more likely to think that something was wrong with you? Would you wonder if God had made a mistake?

SUMMARY

A very normal part of being in a family is dealing with each other's differences. Some degree of conflict is inevitable in any relationship. Clashes between different personality types is to be expected. But when we understand personality type, when we understand the different relational languages God has given us, we can significantly decrease the unnecessary conflicts and misunderstandings.

With the insights of personality type, we are less likely to spend time trying to squeeze our children into our own mold, and more likely to raise them to become the unique people God designed them to be.

In this chapter we've just scratched the surface, introducing the most important aspects of personality type as identified by Meyers-Briggs Type Indicator. However, even with this brief overview, I'm sure you can see how invaluable these insights can be to understanding your children and communicating to them in meaningful ways.

As parents, we have the greatest influence on how our younger children learn, how they understand themselves and others, and how well they grow according to their God-given design. The differences in personality type appear to profoundly affect a child's learning style and developmental pattern.

You can become aware of how your own personality preferences and expectations either blend or clash with those of your children. You can learn how to speak your child's language and increase the probability of clear communication. If you understand some of the most important personality differences between you and your children, you are more likely to nurture them.

DISCOVER YOUR CHILD'S PERSONALITY TYPE

Now that you have a clearer understanding of the basic categories of personality type, it might be helpful for you to take a look at your child's preferences. Keep in mind that a child's personality is still developing, and while some children's preferences may be perfectly clear, others might be ambiguous.

Finding Your Child's Type
Taken from *One of a Kind* by LaVonne Neff

If your children are younger or if you do not want them to take a type indicator, simply observe them. What do you see?

1. Does your child . . .
_____ act quickly, sometimes without thinking?
_____ get tired of long, slow jobs or games?
_____ enjoy learning by doing?
_____ chatter?
_____ enjoy new activities?
_____ want to do things with others?
_____ care what other children think?
_____ unload emotions as they occur?

These are all characteristics of extroverts. When your child does these things, he or she is extroverting.

2. Does your child . . .

___ think before acting?

___ work or play patiently for long periods of time?

___ enjoy learning by reading?

___ keep things to himself or herself?

___ hesitate to try something new?

___ have a few close friends?

___ want a quiet space to work or play in?

___ set his or her own standards despite others' opinions?

___ bottle up emotions?

These are all characteristics of introverts. When your child does these things, he or she is introverting.

3. Does your child . . .

___ enjoy familiar activities and routine?

___ want to know the right way to do things?

___ observe carefully and remember lots of details?

___ memorize easily?

___ ask, "Did it really happen?"

___ like coloring books?

___ enjoy collecting things?

___ enjoy working with his or her hands?

___ seem steady and patient?

These are all characteristics of sensing types. When your child does these things, he or she is perceiving through the senses.

4. Does your child . . .

___ enjoy learning new things?

___ enjoy being different?

___ learn quickly but forget details?

___ have a vivid imagination?

___ enjoy imaginative stories?

___ use toys in new and original ways?

___ often lose things?

___ quickly go from one new interest to another?

___ work and play in fits and starts?

These are all characteristics of intuitive types. When your child does these things, he or she is perceiving through the intuition.

5. Does your child . . .
____ ask "Why?" a lot?
____ insist on logical explanations?
____ get alarmed if someone is treated unfairly?
____ like to arrange things in orderly patterns?
____ show more interest in ideas than in people?
____ hold firmly to his or her beliefs?
____ seem uncomfortable with affection?
____ want rules in games established and kept?
____ like to be praised for doing something competently?

These are all characteristics of thinking types. When your child does these things, he or she is making thinking judgments.

6. Does your child . . .
____ like to talk or read about people?
____ want to be praised for caring for others?
____ get alarmed if someone is unhappy?
____ tell stories expressively, in great detail?
____ try to be tactful, even if that means lying?
____ show more interest in people than in ideas?
____ generally agree with his or her friends' opinions?
____ want to be told you love him or her?
____ relate well to other children, teachers, relatives?

These are all characteristics of feeling types. When your child does these things, he or she is making feeling judgments.

7. Does your child . . .
____ like to know what is going to happen?
____ know how things "ought to be"?
____ enjoy making choices?
____ usually work before playing?
____ discipline himself or herself?
____ have definite goals?
____ have strong opinions?
____ keep a well-ordered room?
____ want to be in charge?

These are all characteristics of judging types. When your child does these things, he or she is relating to the world through his or her judging function.[9]

8. Does your child . . .

_____ enjoy spontaneity?

_____ show a lot of curiosity?

_____ enjoy sampling new experiences and ideas?

_____ turn work into play?

_____ overextend himself or herself?

_____ adapt well to changing circumstances?

_____ keep an open mind?

_____ not object to having things out of place?

_____ want to understand whatever's happening?

These are all characteristics of perceiving types. When your child does these things, he or she is relating to the world through his or her perceiving function.[9]

DELVING DEEPER

The most accurate way to identify your personality type is for you to take the Myers-Briggs Type Indicator (MBTI) or have your children take the Murphy-Meisgeier Type Indicator for Children (MMTIC). To find out who in your area is qualified to give it, ask your pastor or a Christian counselor. Or you can contact the Association for Psychological Type (APT), P.O. Box 5099, Gainesville, FL 32602, (904) 371-1853, and they will put you in touch with someone who can be of help to you.

CHARACTERISTICS FREQUENTLY ASSOCIATED WITH EACH TYPE

Sensing Types

Introverts

ISTJ
Serious, quiet, earn success by concentration and thoroughness. Practical, orderly, matter-of-fact, logical, realistic, and dependable. See to it that everything is well organized. Take responsibility. Make up their own minds as to what should be accomplished and work toward it steadily, regardless of protests or distractions.

ISFJ
Quiet, friendly, responsible, and conscientious. Work devotedly to meet their obligations. Lend stability to any project or group. Thorough, painstaking, accurate. Their interests are usually not technical. Can be patient with necessary details. Loyal, considerate, perceptive, concerned with how other people feel.

ISTP
Cool onlookers — quiet, reserved, observing and analyzing life with detached curiosity and unexpected flashes of original humor. Usually interested in cause and effect, how and why mechanical things work, and in organizing facts using logical principles.

ISFP
Retiring, quiet, friendly, sensitive, kind, modest about their abilities. Shun disagreements, do not force their opinions or values on others. Usually do not care to lead, but are often loyal followers. Often relaxed about getting things done because they enjoy the present moment and do not want to spoil it by undue haste or exertion.

Extroverts

ESTP
Good at on-the-spot problem solving. Do not worry, enjoy whatever comes along. Tend to like mechanical things and sports, with friends on the side. Adaptable, tolerant, generally conservative in values. Dislike long explanations. Are best with real things that can be worked, handled, taken apart, or put together.

ESFP
Outgoing, easygoing, accepting, friendly, enjoy everything and make things more fun for others by their enjoyment. Like sports and making things happen. Know what's going on and join in eagerly. Find remembering facts easier than mastering theories. Are best in situations that need sound common sense and practical ability with people as well as with things.

ESTJ
Practical, realistic, matter-of-fact with a natural head for business or mechanics. Not interested in subjects they see no use for, but can apply themselves when necessary. Like to organize and run activities. May make good administrators, especially if they remember to consider others' feelings and points of view.

ESFJ
Warm-hearted, talkative, popular, conscientious open cooperators, active committee members. Need harmony and may be good at creating it. Always doing something nice for someone. Work best with encouragement and praise. Main interest is in things that directly and visibly affect people's lives.

Intuitive Types

INFJ

Succeed by perseverance, originality, and desire to do whatever is needed or wanted. Put their best efforts into their work. Quietly forceful, conscientious, concerned for others. Respected for their firm principles. Likely to be honored and followed for their clear convictions as to how best to serve the common good.

INTJ

Usually have original minds and great drive for their own ideas and purposes. In fields that appeal to them, they have a fine power to organize a job and carry it through with or without help. Skeptical, critical, independent, determined, sometimes stubborn. Must learn to yield less important points in order to win the most important.

INFP

Full of enthusiasms and loyalties, but seldom talk of these until they know you well. Care about learning ideas, language, and independent projects of their own. Tend to undertake too much, then somehow get it done. Friendly, but often too absorbed in what they are doing to be social. Quite concerned with possessions or physical surroundings.

INTP

Quiet and reserved. Especially enjoy theoretical or scientific pursuits. Like solving problems with logic and analysis. Usually interested mainly in ideas, with little liking for parties or small talk. Tend to have sharply defined interests. Need careers where some strong interest can be used and useful.

ENFP

Warm, enthusiastic, high-spirited, ingenious, imaginative. Able to do most anything that interests them. Quick with a solution for any difficulty and ready to help anyone with a problem. Often rely on their ability to improvise instead of preparing in advance. Can usually find compelling reasons for whatever they want.

ENTP

Quick, ingenious, good at many things. Stimulating company, alert, and outspoken. May argue for fun on either side of a question. Resourceful in solving new and challenging problems, but may neglect routine assignments. Apt to turn to one new interest after another. Skillful in finding logical reasons for what they want.

ENFJ

Responsive and responsible. Generally feel real concern for what others think or want, and try to handle things with due regard for the other person's feelings. Can present a proposal or head a group discussion with ease and tact. Sociable, popular, sympathetic. Responsive to praise and criticism.

ENTJ

Hearty, frank, decisive, leaders in activities. Usually good in anything that requires reasoning and intelligent talk, such as public speaking. Are usually well informed and enjoy adding to their fund of knowledge. May sometimes appear more positive and confident than their experience in an area warrants.

Dealing with emotions that tend to be especially problematic.

Practical principles and responses.

Dealing with Depression

Ted just isn't behaving like a healthy nine-year-old. He's been spending more and more time in his room, either lying on his bed or watching TV. Every now and then he'll complain about being bored, but when someone invites him to play, he refuses. Whenever his parents say something to encourage him, he responds with, "Yeah, sure. If you only knew!"

What's wrong with Ted? Ted is depressed. Yes, even children become depressed.

You may be surprised at the most recent information concerning children and depression. Studies have shown that one out of four children in our country has some type of psychiatric disorder. And as research results continue to be released from the National Institute of Mental Health, the conclusion is that most adults with mood or anxiety problems developed these problems in their childhood.

Fred is an active three-year-old (at least until last week). Now, he just seems to mope around with a long face. He shows no interest regardless of his mother's efforts to involve him in play. He's not ill—he just doesn't seem to care anymore.

Can toddlers become depressed? Just a few years ago specialists realized that preschoolers could experience true depressive feelings. Since young children are unable to verbalize their emotions clearly, parents often excuse listless or tearful episodes as the normal ups and downs of growing up.[1] But the fact is that even newborns can show signs of being depressed. It's just very difficult to diagnose.

How common is depression among young children? A recent study indicated that as many as 8 percent of preschool-age children experience significant depression, and as they get older, their chances of becoming depressed actually increase.[2]

Most depression in childhood goes away quickly, but some kids suffer from the more serious, disabling type of depression as well. This chronic type of depression seems to evolve for no apparent reason, or it is out of proportion to whatever it is that set it off.

The difficulty is that even concerned parents can be so distracted by their own marriages, occupations, or daily responsibilities that they miss the warning signals of their depressed child. They also don't recognize the events that can trigger depression.

WHY DO CHILDREN BECOME DEPRESSED?

Many factors can trigger depression in a child. Some of the more common culprits are:
- a physical defect or illness;
- malfunction of the endocrine glands;
- a lack of affection, creating insecurity;
- a lack of positive feedback or encouragement;
- death of a parent;
- divorce, separation, or parental desertion;
- sibling favoritism;
- relationship problems between child and stepparent;
- financial problems in the family;
- a sensitivity to punishment; and
- a move or change of schools.[3]

Also, behavioral experts have found that certain personality types have a predisposition to depression. While some children take certain events in stride, another child crumbles and falls into depression. A child who is highly sensitive, lacks assertiveness, tends to hide his or her feelings, and has a low self-esteem is particularly vulnerable to depression.

Children often become depressed because of a loss. Sudden loss is particularly hard on children, leaving them feeling out-of-control and floundering. On the other hand, a gradual loss that can be prepared for is easier for children to manage.

Often depression is heightened if what is lost is perceived as necessary and irreplaceable. In his book on depression, Dr. Archibald Hart describes four different types of loss:

Abstract losses are intangible, such as the loss of self-respect, love, hope, or ambition. Our mind perceives these losses, and we feel we have experienced them. At times the loss may be real, but it may not be as bad as we feel it is.

Concrete losses involve tangible objects—a home, a car, a parent, a close friend, a photograph, or a pet. We could feel and see the object prior to the loss.

Imagined losses are created solely by our active imaginations. We think someone doesn't like us anymore. We think people are talking behind our backs. Children often excel at this. Their self-talk focuses on negatives and may not be based on fact.

The most difficult type of loss to handle, however, is the *threatened loss*. This loss has not yet occurred, but there is the real possibility that it will happen. To a child, waiting for the results of a physical exam, or waiting to hear from his relatives to see if he can go to their farm for the summer, carries the possibility of loss. Depression occurs because, in this type of loss, the child is powerless to do anything about it. In a sense, he is immobilized.[4]

SIGNS OF DEPRESSION

What does a depressed child look like? How can parents know if their child is really depressed and not just sad about something that has happened? We first need to understand the distinction between depression and sadness. The feeling of sadness is less intense than that of depression; it doesn't last as long, nor does it interfere with day-to-day functioning. Depression causes us to function at 50 percent of normal, and this lower functioning level intensifies our feelings of depression. That's a key sign.

A depressed child feels empty. He cannot fully understand the meaning of life nor the void within himself, but he does know that something is wrong.

Below is a composite of the depressed child. Your child probably won't display all of these symptoms:

1. Your child may appear sad or depressed. We call this apathy, and it can be expressed in several ways. The child might appear restless but doesn't become involved in activity, may decline to do things he or she usually enjoys, preferring to be alone to just daydream. Apathy in a child is a symptom of internal stress.

2. A prominent feature of childhood depression is withdrawal and inhibition. We call this listlessness. The child may look bored, or often even appears to be ill.

3. A depressed child may display physical symptoms, often complaining of headaches, stomachaches, dizziness, insomnia, or eating and sleeping disturbances. These symptoms are called depressive equivalents.

4. A depressed child looks discontented and seems to experience very little pleasure from life.

5. Many depressed children feel rejected and unloved. They withdraw from any situation that may disappoint them. They fear and expect rejection and protect themselves from it.

Depressed children feel unimportant. The method of expression differs from child to child, but depressed children feel they are less valuable than other children. These feelings of inadequacy and low self-esteem may appear in the following ways:

- Quitting a club or ball team because he sees himself as insignificant. ("They'll never miss me.")
- Failing to reach out to help others for fear of rejection. ("She doesn't want my help.")
- Rejecting affection because of a feeling of unworthiness. ("She can't really love me.")

- Deliberately breaking rules because he thinks following them will lead to failure. ("Others expect too much of me. They won't like it when I fail.")
- Failing to recognize that mistakes and failures can be corrected. ("I'll never get it right.")
- Refusing to admit to a mistake or failure to save face. ("Why do I always lose?")
- Rejecting the need to learn or grow. ("What difference will it make if I know that or not?")
- Unwillingness to share with others. ("I rarely get anything worthwhile, so why should I share it? I'm going to keep it all for me.")
- Blaming others for difficulties and problems. ("Others try to make my life hard.")
- Rejecting spiritual teachings that could help. ("Why would God love me? I don't believe it.")[5]

6. When the depressed child speaks, she's negative about herself and everything in her life. She draws conclusions based on her negative mind-set rather than on fact. This further reinforces her feelings of depression.

7. A depressed child will show unusual levels of frustration and irritability. When this child fails to reach his goals, he will be especially hard on himself, commenting disparagingly about his abilities and value.

8. A depressed child looks for comfort and support from others, but when she receives it, refuses to be comforted and encouraged.

9. Some children will mask their feelings of despair by clowning and acting foolish. Provocative children are less likely to appear in need of comfort and support, so the depression can continue undetected.

10. Some children demonstrate drastic mood swings when depressed. One minute they appear to be "up" and the next minute they're in the pit of despair. These children tend to believe that if they are "good" enough and work hard enough, that life will turn around for them.

11. The depressed child may become the family scapegoat. His behavior can elicit anger and parents might label him a "problem child." With this label, the depression continues and

the child may begin to live up to this classification.

12. The depressed child may tend to be passive, excessively dependent, and assume parents automatically know her needs. Since it's impossible to read a child's thoughts, her needs go unmet. She may become angry and respond in passive aggressive ways.

13. Depressed kids tend to be overly sensitive, hard on themselves, and self-critical. They create unreasonable goals for themselves, and blame themselves when they fail to attain them.

14. Some depressed children will become regressive and obsessive in order to cope with how badly they feel.

Depressed kids won't exhibit all of these characteristics, but when some of them exist, don't just assume the child is misbehaving.[6]

Many children experience depression because they are having difficulties dealing with other people. The strongest need a child has is to belong—to be part of a family and social group. Children who are having problems developing positive relationships are in crisis and can become depressed.

Depression can also result from a traumatic incident. In such cases, the depressed feelings are usually short-lived, and the child soon returns to normal. Following are situations that may not be bothersome to us as adults, but can cause temporary depression in a child.

- Failing an exam or a class.
- Being overlooked for a desired position.
- Performing poorly in an organized activity such as Little League, T-ball, or gymnastics.
- Unable to find someone with whom to play.
- Being reprimanded or punished.
- Arguing with a parent, sibling, or friend.
- Losing a favorite object or a pet.
- Being denied a request.
- Entering puberty.
- Moving from one home to another or losing friends.

While these situations cause only short-term depression, circumstances that seem to have no end can leave a child emotionally drained and less resilient. Following are situations that

can generate long-term depression in a child.
- Constant arguments within the family.
- Obvious marital problems between parents.
- Lack of one-on-one communication.
- Frequent criticism.
- Conditional love—affection and positive attention based on performance.
- Financial pressures.
- Substance abuse within the family.
- Inadequate and inconsistent discipline.
- Limited social and intellectual stimulation.
- Difficult socialization with peers.
- Lack of success caused by learning problems.

A depression-prone child can interpret a parent's response as a reinforcement of his negative worth. For example:
- Frequent criticism.
Your child's interpretation: "I can't do anything right."
- Lack of individual attention from parent.
Your child's interpretation: "I'm not important."
- Harsh or angry words from parents.
Your child's interpretation: "I make others feel upset."
- Parents' failure to acknowledge accomplishments.
Your child's interpretation: "The things I do don't count."
- Parents focusing on negative or upsetting behavior.
Your child's interpretation: "Everyone expects me to be bad."
- Parents' failure to keep promises.
Your child's interpretation: "No one cares if I'm disappointed."

Over time, continuous negative experiences like these contribute to feelings of low self-worth which lead to depressed feelings.[7]

HOW PARENTS CAN HELP THEIR DEPRESSED KIDS

Most parents don't know what to do for their depressed kids. What can you say to your depressed child?

Seven-year-old Katy would begin to cry at the drop of a hat. She constantly made negative statements about herself. She talked about being ugly (which was far from the truth), how others didn't like her (her friends called every day), and how she couldn't do anything right (she was a straight-A student). This has been going on for a month. No matter what her parents say or do, she seems to get worse rather than better.

How should Katy's parents respond to her? What can they say to her? What can they do to help Katy get through this time?

A good place to start is by communicating that they care for Katy, want to be with her, and will be available to her.

Conveying acceptance is also important. There is healing in physical touch. An arm around your child's shoulder, a pat on the back, or holding your child's hand can communicate comfort and acceptance. But by all means, be honest and tell your child, "I don't really understand all that you're going through, but I'm trying—and I'm here to help you."

Here are some practical quidelines to help you understand and deal with the problem of depression. How closely you follow these will depend upon the intensity and duration of the depression. If your child is experiencing short-term depression and still functioning, certain suggestions will not apply. However, if the depression has lasted quite a while and your child is not eating, sleeping, or functioning on a normal level, you will apply more of these guidelines to the situation.

1. Help your child learn to express depressed feelings.

Keep in mind that depression robs people of the ability to govern their thinking and emotions. If your depressed child just stares, ignores greetings, or turns away from you, remember that he doesn't want to act that way. He's not trying to punish you. A severely depressed child can't control himself any more than you could walk a straight line after twirling around 25 times.

Your child needs to talk about the problems that depress her, but she may avoid doing so. Why? She may think you're not interested—that her problems will seem insignificant to you—or it may be difficult for her to bring up the topic. This is when your availability becomes crucial to your child's survival. Enough time needs to be spent with your child to allow for informal talks that open the door to more serious discussions.

When your child does begin to talk about his or her feelings, several important guidelines should be followed. They are:

- Understand what is being said from your child's point of view. His interpretation of matters (which might be considerably different from yours) is important since his beliefs will largely determine future behavior.
- Your nonverbal expressions should indicate a genuine interest in what your child is saying. Avoid anything that might distract you from focusing directly on your child.
- Use questions to gather information from your child. Avoid implying wrongdoing or guilt in your tone.
- Withhold giving your opinions, information, or advice until your child is ready and open for assistance. Let your child decide whether you will listen or offer suggestions.
- Control your own emotions. It will help your child maintain composure. A power struggle at this point could serve to just intensify your child's feelings.
- Don't try to fill every moment with words. Silence can allow your child to organize his thoughts.
- Watch your child's nonverbal expressions. Look for the feelings that lie beneath your child's words.
- Allow for disagreement. Your child's perspective may be different than yours.[8]

2. Watch out for the possibility of suicide.

The family of a depressed person should be aware of the possibility of suicide. It may shock you, but any suspicions of suicide should be taken seriously. Unfortunately, the incidence of suicide is on the rise, and a child who expresses utter hopelessness for the future may be at risk. If the child is able to talk about his suicidal thoughts or plans, it helps bring them out into the open as well as solicit your support and help.

3. Consult with your pediatrician.

Certain physical problems can cause depressed feelings. When a child suffers from long-term depression, it's important to consult your pediatrician for possible causes and treatments.

4. Give support and make adjustments.

The whole family needs to be informed and coached when one of its members is depressed. Ask each person to avoid conflicts, put-downs, and unrealistic expectations until things are back to normal. Confrontation and strong discipline should be suspended until stability is restored.

5. Don't avoid the depressed child.

Avoiding the depressed child further isolates her and worsens the problem. Don't allow yourself to feel guilty and somehow responsible for her depression. Remember that, while someone may contribute to another's problems from time to time, no one person is responsible for another's happiness.

6. Realize that a depressed child is a hurting child.

Don't tell a depressed child to "just snap out of it." Avoid offering simple solutions like "Just pray about it" or "Read your Bible more." And never imply that a child is using depression to solicit sympathy. To a depressed child, emotional pain is as intense—if not more intense—as physical pain.

7. Empathize rather than sympathize with your child.

Sympathy only reinforces someone's feelings of hopelessness. Statements such as "It's awful that you're depressed" and "You must feel miserable" tend to encourage helplessness and low self-esteem. Instead, let the child know you've had similar experiences and you know these feelings will pass.

8. Reconstruct your child's self-esteem.

One of the most important steps a parent can take is to help rebuild a child's self-esteem, because when depression occurs, self-esteem tends to crumble. A depressed child doesn't understand his value as God's creation and the extent of God's love for him. Because of this, he doubts everyone's love as well.

Because a depressed child is unwilling to participate in normal activity, it won't be easy to involve her in opportunities that reinforce self-worth. It might be better to just get the child involved without a lot of discussion. Involve him in activities you know he enjoys—and in which he has experienced success. Focus his attention on his accomplishments. Don't let your child's apathy discourage you. Remember, your child is cautious right now and lacks enthusiasm for life. In time, his excitement and enthusiasm will return.[9]

9. Watch your child's diet.

A depressed child may have no appetite, but nutrition is still important. Don't let food become another "issue" by harping on it or using guilt to get your child to eat. Instead, explain to your child that, hungry or not, it's important to eat. Sit with your child and try to make mealtimes an enjoyable family event.

10. Keep your child busy.

To the severely depressed child, physical activity is more beneficial than mental activity. Your child's behavior will tend to reinforce his depression by avoiding others, withdrawing from normal activities, not eating well, and offending friends. For this reason, you may run into resistance, so you'll need to take charge of planning your child's activities. If he's lost interest in things he usually enjoys, remind him of the fun he's had in the past, and then gently but firmly insist that he become involved. Don't ask him if he wants to do something—he'll probably decline. And don't allow yourself to become frustrated and say something like, "You're going with me because I'm sick and tired of you feeling sorry for yourself." Instead, you might say something like, "I know you haven't been feeling well, but you are entitled to some fun. I think you might like this once we get started. I would like to share this activity with you."

Use any activity your child enjoys, but be aware that you may need to schedule his entire day for him. But by getting him involved, you help him begin to break destructive behavior patterns and gain energy and motivation.

11. Never tease or belittle your child for a lack of self-confidence.

Neither showcase nor ignore a low self-esteem. It is a common problem of depression and must be faced. Don't argue about or participate in your child's self-pity, but present the illogical nature of her self-disparagement. Remind her of past accomplishments and help her focus on her abilities. If she says, "I can't do anything," gently name her skills and talents. In time, as her confidence builds, she will begin to overcome her sense of helplessness.

SUMMARY

Be persistent and consistent in responding to your children's depression. Remember, they are not in control emotionally, but you are. If they remain unresponsive or if the depression is severe, you should seek professional help. But by following these principles and using common sense, parents can do a lot to help their children through the depressive periods of their young lives.[10]

Dealing with Anger

"I've had it. I give up. I quit," Perry said in quiet desperation. "I've tried everything I can think of to help Tyler with his anger. Nothing seems to work. The harder I try, the more he resists. I hate to admit it, but the more he resists, the more frustrated I get. When my frustration reaches a certain point, I lose it. And then I feel guilty because I'm modeling the very thing I don't want him to do."

Perry is a sensitive and gracious man who loves the Lord, his wife, and his children. He really wants to be a good dad, but all his life he's struggled with the emotion of anger.

He's not the only one. Both his father and his grandfather had problems dealing with anger as well. When Perry and Karen's first child was born, Perry's prayer was that he would help his children learn to deal with their anger. He didn't want to model what he'd seen as a child. That's why his struggle with Tyler was especially frustrating and discouraging.

In our work with families, we've discovered that, of all the emotions God gave us, anger is the most difficult to deal with. Parents struggle more with their own anger than with any other emotion. They also report having more difficulty dealing with their children's anger.

Nancy Samalin expresses what Perry is experiencing and what I've heard hundreds of parents express:

> For many families, home is a battleground, filled with constant bickering, shouting matches, and exhausting power struggles. Often, parents' complaints appear so frivolous they hardly seem worth the effort of doing battle over. Parents are amazed that they can go from relative calm to utter frustration in a few seconds. An uneaten egg or spilled juice at breakfast can turn a calm morning into a free-for-all. In spite of parents' best intentions, bedtime becomes wartime, meals end with children in tears and food barely touched, and car rides deteriorate into stress-filled shouting matches. . . . Whatever its source, we often experience parental anger as a horrifying encounter with our worst selves. I never even knew I had a temper until I had children. It was very frightening that these children I loved so much, for whom I had sacrificed so much, could arouse such intense feelings of rage in me, their mother, whose primary responsibility was to nurture and protect them.[1]

I don't know about you, but most parents I've talked with can easily relate to that statement. Why is anger so difficult for parents to deal with? What's unique about anger that makes it such a problem?

UNDERSTANDING ANGER

Anger is the most misunderstood of all the emotions. It's important for us to know that anger isn't really the problem. The problem is our misconceptions about anger. To properly understand anger, we must discover why God has given it to us and how we can use it in constructive ways to achieve our goals.

Let's face it, anger has a bad reputation. In fact, many Christians have the notion that anger is sinful. Why is it that people have such a negative opinion of anger?

What exactly is anger? What are some of the words that come to mind when you think of anger? A few might be rage, fury, wrath, resentment, and hostility. Webster defines anger as "emotional excitement induced by intense displeasure." Anger is a strong feeling of irritation or displeasure. It is also energy.

If we are going to help our children understand and deal with this strong emotion, there are a few things we need to understand about anger.

1. Anger is a God-given emotion.

The one single thing that makes being human unique is that we are created in God's image. That means we will experience a variety of our own as well as others' emotions.

One of these emotions is anger. From Genesis 4:5 through Revelation 19:15, the Bible has a lot to say about anger. In fact, in the Old Testament alone, anger is mentioned approximately 455 times with 375 of those passages referring specifically to God's anger.

2. Anger creates a physical state of readiness.

When we become angry, our minds and bodies prepare us to act. Anger creates physical and emotional energy. That energy can be used in a positive way to right wrongs and change things for the good. But misdirected, it can lead to emotional, verbal, and even physical abuse.

Unfortunately, many people believe that, because anger is such a powerful emotion, it can't be controlled and must be avoided at all cost. These people have learned to deny, suppress, repress, and ignore their anger. They don't understand its power so they don't know how to deal with it constructively. The problem is not the anger itself but rather our inability to make it work for us.

People often confuse the emotion of anger with some of the unhealthy and irresponsible ways it is expressed—they confuse anger with aggression. But they're not the same. Anger is an emotion, aggression is an action. Anger is often associated with rage. But there's an important difference. Rage is anger out of control. The problem is not the emotion of anger but rather the way it is expressed.

When our children have been hurt or wronged, they will experience anger. Their first instinct will be to seek revenge.

Their ability to see the situation clearly will be limited because anger distorts their perspective. If they don't learn to experience and express their anger appropriately, the consequences can be devastating.

Remember, anger is energy. Our kids can choose to either spend it or invest. A parent's job is to teach children to harness and channel that energy in healthy, positive, and constructive ways. As they learn creative ways to invest this God-given energy, develop effective anger management skills, and approach anger from a biblical perspective, they will discover the most powerful source of motivation available to mankind.

3. Anger is a secondary emotion.

Anger is always a response to another emotion or combination of emotions. Many factors can contribute to anger, but we've found that the primary causes are hurt, frustration, and fear.

Hurt is usually caused by something that has happened in the past. It makes us feel vulnerable and open to further hurt. This is especially true of very sensitive kids.

David and Daniel are eight-year-old twins. David is especially sensitive. While Daniel is also sensitive, he has learned to let things roll off him.

One day David came home from school and stormed into the house steaming mad. "Carl was making fun of us on the bus," he fumed. "I hate him. If he does it again tomorrow, I'm going to hit him right in the face."

When his mom asked Daniel about what happened, he replied, "Carl makes fun of everyone. It's no big deal. If you just ignore him, he goes away." Two kids with the exact same situation and two different ways of responding. David personalized what Carl had said and experienced hurt. Anger is probably our most automatic defense mechanism—protecting us from hurt. It builds a wall of protection around us. Some people learn to feel safer hiding behind that wall, and it becomes an unhealthy expression that puts distance between individuals.

Another unhealthy way to deal with hurt is to not acknowledge or respond to it. Unattended hurt turns to bitterness and resentment that can flare up into aggression, rage, and violence. That's what happened in Genesis 37. Jacob's favoritism with Joseph caused his brothers to be jealous. Joseph's brothers sat on their hurt feelings until they turned into murderous thoughts. Scripture says that they plotted against him to put him to death.

Frustration is an emotion that takes place in the present. We become frustrated by blocked goals, desires, and unmet expectations. It's especially easy for children to become frustrated. Their young bodies are developing, and they can feel awkward at times. Their minds are also developing and there's much they don't yet understand. Young children are particularly vulnerable to frustration because they don't have a memory bank of similar experiences against which to evaluate and compare their current experiences. The present is all there is.

Frequently, the things that cause frustration aren't very important, but they appear to be of major significance to the child.

Joyce had been working hard building a tower with her Legos. She was trying to balance a large section of blocks on top of a narrow tower she had erected. It kept falling off. After the third try, she threw the section across the room, frantically tore apart what she'd already made, and stormed out of the room. "I'm never going to play with those stupid Legos again."

It's important to identify sources of frustration. What are the situations that cause your children to become frustrated? Which individuals frustrate them more than others? When are they most vulnerable to experiencing frustration? How do they respond when they're feeling frustrated?

Fear is an emotion that tends to focus on the future. Many people associate fear with vulnerability and weakness. Men especially find it more comfortable to express anger than fear, so they tend to respond angrily when anxious or afraid.

Tim heard his seven-year-old sister coming up the stairs and thought it would be a great idea to hide behind the door and scare her when she walked into the room. When Linda walked into the room, he did a masterful job of jumping out from behind the door with a blood-curdling scream. Linda's first response was to scream. Her next response was to kick Tim, run downstairs, and tell Mom that Tim was being mean. Tim hadn't even touched Linda, but he'd activated her fear which triggered anger.

When one of your children is experiencing anger, ask yourself if the source of that anger is hurt, frustration, fear, or a combination of all three.

4. Anger may be difficult to identify.
Anger may be difficult to identify because it can be disguised as:
- criticism
- silence
- intimidation
- hypochondria
- depression
- petty complaints
- gossip and blame
- stubbornness
- halfhearted efforts
- forgetfulness
- laziness

An important step in helping our children understand their anger is to study them and discover the ways they experience and express their anger.

5. People don't want to admit to being angry.
Most people have a hard time admitting they are angry. For some reason, this is especially true in evangelical circles. Perhaps it's because anger has mistakenly been labeled as sin.

Let your children know when you're experiencing anger. Let them hear you say, "I'm angry."

6. Anger can be healthy or unhealthy.
Healthy anger is usually moderate in intensity. It has not progressed to rage. It doesn't consume us. We're not overwhelmed by it. Healthy anger can help us attain our goals.

Unhealthy anger consumes us. It is in control. It distorts our perspective, robs us of energy, blurs our focus, and creates turmoil. Unhealthy anger can become abusive, violent, and destructive.

7. Anger is a positive emotion.
The positive side of anger has not been emphasized in the Christian community. Anger has tremendous potential for

good. It can signal that something is wrong. It can alert us to danger and warn us when our rights are being violated. Anger can provide us with immediate energy to deal with a crisis or take constructive action to right a wrong.

For most people, the emotion of anger is considered negative—a problem to be eliminated or solved. What we often fail to see is that every problem is an opportunity in disguise—an opportunity to learn, grow, mature, and to be used of God to make significant changes in our lives.

WHAT TO DO BEFORE YOUR CHILD GETS ANGRY

I've talked with many parents who want to know what they can do once their child is angry. But that's not the place to begin. The best time to help your child deal with his anger is before he gets angry.

One of the most helpful things a parent can do is to normalize the emotion of anger. Talk about emotions with your children. Help them understand what emotions are and where they come from. Make sure they know that emotions aren't good or bad, right or wrong.

It's natural for children to experience joy, surprise, delight, fear, hurt, frustration, disappointment, discouragement, depression, and anger. Teach them how to identify and name their emotions. Ask them what they are feeling. Help them develop a vocabulary for their emotional lives. This makes it easier for them to understand their own emotional lives as well as talk about them with you.

Let your kids know that you are encouraged when they identify their anger. This suggests that they are growing in their understanding of their emotions. It indicates that they are learning how to deal with this powerful emotion in healthy kinds of ways.

Carrie and I have worked with each one of our three sons to help them name their emotions. One evening we had company, and our son Matthew came up and asked if he could talk to me. I excused myself from a conversation, lowered myself so that we were eye-to-eye, and asked him what was up.

"Dad," he said, "I'm angry."

My first response was, "That's great." But as I said it, I realized that it might be confusing to him so I added, "I'm glad that you know when you are angry and that you want to talk about it."

His ability to identify and label his emotion made it much easier to help him deal with a difficult situation and express his anger in a constructive rather than a destructive way.

1. Make use of resources.

The library is a good resource for teaching your children about emotions. It has a variety of secular and Christian books that deal with various aspects of children's emotions. As kids read about other children's experiences, parents will find opportunities to talk about emotions. You can start discussions by asking questions like, "Honey, have you ever felt like that?" Or, "Do you remember the last time you experienced anger?" Stories provide children with alternative ways to understand and deal with their own experiences. Many children find it easier to learn from other children's experiences than from an adult's experience.

2. Create the right atmosphere for healthy emotions.

Make sure your home is a place where it is safe for your children to experience and express a wide range of emotions. Let them know that in your family it is OK to be angry. At the same time, let them know that there are acceptable and unacceptable ways to express that anger. Make sure they know what the unacceptable expressions are and what the consequences will be when they choose to respond in those ways.

3. Check the environmental balance in your home.

Make sure your child's environment isn't a setup for anger. Monitor their nutrition and make sure they get plenty of rest. Be aware of their schedules and the pressures they face. It's amazing how busy many children's lives can become. The challenges, expectations, demands continue to grow. Most of us are vulnerable to frustration when we get tired. We can eliminate a lot of unnecessary frustration and pain from our families by making periodic environmental adjustments.

4. Know your children.

Study each of your children. When are they most likely to experience anger? What kinds of situations increase the probability that they will get angry? How do they usually express that anger? What is the most effective way to communicate with them when they are angry?

5. Be thankful for anger.

Pray with your children about their emotions. Talk about their emotions with them, and then thank God for the gift of our emotions. Don't leave out the gift of anger. As you thank God for anger, thank Him for the specific positive things that can come from our anger. If you have seen your child respond to anger in a positive way, thank God for what he or she is learning about his or her anger.

6. Model healthy anger.

Be aware of what you model for your children. Watch your verbal and nonverbal communication when you discipline them. What is your immediate reaction when your child has an angry outburst? If you are like most parents, you want to shut it down. I've heard countless parents, including myself, respond with statements such as, "You shouldn't be angry. There's no reason to get mad. I'm sick and tired of arguing with you. If you don't stop it right now, I'm really going to get mad." What do these kinds of statements teach our children about anger?

7. Talk about your own anger.

When you are angry with your children or someone else, say, "I'm angry." If you are angry with your children and are concerned that the emotion is controlling you rather than you controlling it, tell them that you need to take time out to process your anger. On several occasions I've told one of my kids, "I'm experiencing a lot of anger right now, but I need to take a few minutes to cool down and think about it. I'll be back in a few minutes, and we'll talk about the consequences for what you've done."

8. Major on the majors.

Avoid unnecessary power struggles. Children have more time and energy to resist us than we have to force them to do every little thing we think they should. Even if we do win a battle and get them to do something our way, they may retaliate by becoming spiritless, rebellious, delinquent, or neurotic. The key here is to pick your battles according to your priorities.

HELPING YOUR CHILDREN UNDERSTAND AND DEAL WITH THEIR ANGER

1. Help your children be aware of their anger.

Carl is not considered an angry child. He rarely appears angry. But while Carl does not appear angry on the outside, he is like a battlefield on the inside. If he has had a difficult day at school, he is more quiet when he comes home and tends to isolate himself in his room. He's more likely to be negative and critical of everything and everyone. His mom has learned to watch for these symptoms, and when she sees them, she knows that Carl is angry.

One of the many myths about anger is that if a person doesn't look or appear on the outside to be angry, then he doesn't have a problem with anger—he is clearly not an angry person.

Help your children become aware of how they respond to their anger. How often are you aware of your children being angry? Which situations do they encounter that might make them more vulnerable to anger? How do their bodies respond to anger? What are their physical manifestations of anger? How do they treat others when they are angry? What is unique about the ways in which each of your children experiences and expresses anger?

2. Once they're aware of their anger, help them process it.

When children are feeling overwhelmed by strong emotions, it is tempting for parents to jump in to help them get over it. This is especially true with the emotion of anger. We're tempted to give them advice about what to do.

When kids are in the midst of powerful emotions, they have a hard time listening to anyone. The last thing they want is advice or criticism. They simply want to be heard and understood. They want you to know how they feel. Many times the most effective way to release angry feelings is to just sit down and listen to them.

Make sure to pick the right time to talk with them. Take into account their personality types. Most extroverts like to process things externally. They like to talk about things right away. Most introverts prefer to process things internally. They like to think about it before they talk about it. Being insensitive to your children's preferred way to process their anger could only increase frustration and increase the anger, making it more difficult, if not impossible, to deal with.

In time, you will be able to help your children develop more words for their anger. When your children say, "I'm angry," you can respond by asking, "Do you think your anger is from being afraid, hurt, or frustrated?"

3. Help your children accept responsibility for their anger.

Someone has said that one of the main effects of original sin is seen in our tendency to blame someone else for our problems. When God confronted Eve in the Garden and asked her what happened, she blamed the serpent. When God confronted Adam, he first blamed Eve and then he blamed God.

We can teach our children that when we are angry, it is easy for us to blame someone else—to say, "It's your fault, you made me angry." This is especially true with brothers and sisters. Brothers and sisters have a built-in cause for all of their problems. Over time we can teach our children that, while others say or do things that cause hurt or frustration, we are responsible for how we choose to respond. If we are angry, it is our anger.

4. Help your child decide who or what will have control.

This is a very important step for children and adults. But it's a bit more difficult for children. They haven't had the time to develop some of the discipline and controls that adults have, nor the understanding of consequences. But they have an opportunity to learn discipline and control.

When they become aware that they are angry, we can help them learn that they are faced with a choice. They can either allow anger to dominate and control them or they can, with the help of the Holy Spirit, choose to control the anger and invest the energy in healthy ways.

A simple yet powerful response can be, "Honey, I can tell that you are feeling a lot of anger right now. It's OK to experience anger. I'm glad you're able to talk about it. It sounds like you've got some good reasons to be angry. Now, you need to decide if you are going to let your anger control you or if you want to control it. Do you remember what happened last week when you let your anger get out of control? Is that what you want to happen again? Would you like me to pray with you to ask God to help you deal with your anger in a healthy way?"

The way you talk to your children will depend on their age and individual emotional development. But, however you choose to express it, you can help your kids understand that as soon as they're aware of their anger, they need to decide whether they are going to control their anger and deal with it constructively, or allow their anger to control them and lead to further problems.

5. Help your kids identify the cause of their anger.

Children get angry for many of the same reasons adults get angry. Anger is a normal response to all kinds of daily events that produce fear, hurt, and frustration.

Be careful not to react to your child's anger. Remember that anger is a secondary emotion. Instead, ask yourself where the anger is coming from. What's the real issue? A child's anger is often communicating a need he or she may not be aware of. They may be frightened, sad, insecure, confused—it appears as anger.

Once your child has had time to cool down from an angry outburst, then you can explore the cause of the anger. When you start, your child may be completely unaware of what triggered the angry response. But talking about fear, hurt, insults, disappointments, discouragements, rejection, and frustration will stimulate their awareness and recognition. Take the time to explore with them what's been going on in their lives. Ask questions. Listen. Let them ramble. As you take the time to understand them, you will help them understand themselves and communicate your love, support, and encouragement.

6. Help your children choose their responses and develop their own solutions.

There are many ways to deal with anger—some constructive, some destructive. Destructive ways to deal with anger are to stuff, deny, suppress, or repress. For some, talking about anger only serves to work them up more.

One of the most destructive ways of dealing with anger is to ventilate it or dump it on someone else. Ventilating the anger tends to increase rather than decrease its intensity. That's why it is important for us to help our kids move from a "what's the problem" mode to a "what do you want to do about it" mode.

If we allow our kids to spend too much time wallowing in the muck and mire of the problem, it will only make things worse. It will decrease their energy, increase their feelings of hopelessness and helplessness, and make successful resolution almost impossible.

One way to teach kids to choose healthy responses to their anger is to say, "Now that you know that your anger came from being frustrated with your brother, you can decide what you're going to do about your frustration. What do you think you'd like to do?"

If they don't have any ideas, you could say, "I can think of four different ways you can handle your frustration. If you want to hear them, I'd be happy to share them with you. Think about it and let me know."

As much as possible, it is important to allow children to develop their own solutions to their problems. With younger children, you may have to prime the pump a bit, but as they get older, they will have developed a wide range of their own responses.

7. Help your children review their responses to anger.

Many of us miss this step. After a couple of days have passed, ask your child what he learned about dealing with his anger. What worked well? What does he wish he'd done differently? What would he do differently next time?

This conversation will only take a few minutes. You need to discuss what they learned and not what you as a parent think they should have learned. Don't let it turn into a lecture — that will undermine the process and rob them of a great learning experience.

Remember, learning to understand and deal with emotions is a lifelong process. It takes time. It involves trial and error. But the product is worth the effort. Encourage each step your child takes. Congratulate them whenever possible. Praise them for even making an effort.

WHAT CAN I DO WHEN MY KIDS
FIGHT ALL THE TIME?

"Mom," Nathan screamed, "Matthew got to watch the Turtles, but he won't let me watch Inspector Gadget!" Suddenly, we heard a bloodcurdling scream, and Matthew came running into the kitchen. The scream was so loud and painful that you would've thought a limb had been severed without anesthesia. "Mom, Nathan hit me and I didn't do anything!"

One of the main concerns all parents face is sibling rivalry. Most parents report this as one of the common sources of anger for their children. Whenever children are competing for toys, parental attention, or space, it's normal for them to experience frustration. As kids' frustration increases, so does the parents'. Yet parents need to understand that sibling rivalry provides an excellent opportunity for kids to learn the socializing skills of assertiveness and compromise.[2]

The first principle to keep in mind is to ignore the minor, everyday disagreements. If you try to solve every fight, or figure out who is right and wrong, or who really started it, you will go crazy. You will also rob your kids of the opportunity to develop their own problem-solving skills.

When problems reach a point when you must intervene, do it in such a way that makes your children responsible for solving the problems they have created. Listen to them. Clarify what they are saying. Communicate that you understand. Express your confidence in them to be able to work it out. Teach them how to manage their own arguments. Provide ideas on how they might compromise. Help them generate options, weigh alternatives, and follow through.

Kids need to feel safe. They need to be secure in the fact that you won't leave them unprotected. They need to know that it is never acceptable to hit a brother or sister. They need to understand that there are clear consequences for certain kinds of behavior. If you have these kinds of safety factors in your home, they are more likely to be open to moving into a problem-solving mode than responding in ways that only create more problems.

Parents must learn to ignore the minor disagreements that characterize normal sibling relationships, and intervene only when serious conflicts threaten to get out of control. It takes a lot of practice and a willingness to risk making mistakes to learn how to differentiate between the two. You will make mistakes. You will lose your temper. You will get discouraged. You will wish you could call these authors on the phone and say, "Hey, it's not that easy." And, you're right. It's not easy. But with practice, consistency, and prayer it can be done.

During those times, remember that Romans 8:28 is true. God can cause all things to work together for good—your disappointments, your discouragements, even your mistakes. Being open and honest about your own feelings can be a powerful learning experience for your children. It lets them know that you are human. It shows them in practical ways that what you are telling them really works. When you show them that you can learn from your mistakes, it lets them know that they can learn from theirs too.

TAKE ACTION

How Angry Is Your Child?

Child's Name: _____

The following inventory covers the more common signs of anger in children. All children occasionally manifest these signs, but if several of them are persistent or if your kids evidence many of them, you may have a problem.

Rate each statement according to the following scale and enter the rating in the right column:

0 = My child never or rarely does this.
1 = My child occasionally does this (no more than once a month).
2 = My child often (once a week or so) does this.
3 = My child does this frequently (daily or several times a week).

Rating

1. My child blames others for his or her troubles. _____
2. My child throws or breaks things whenever he or she feels frustrated or irritated. _____
3. Whenever my child gets angry, calming him or her down takes a lot of placating. _____
4. My child does not like change of any sort and becomes angry when change is forced on him or her. _____
5. My child changes the rules of games when playing with other children. _____
6. My child says spiteful or hateful things whenever he or she is thwarted. _____
7. My child is negative, deliberately slow, and resists doing what he or she is told to do to the point that discipline becomes a standoff. _____
8. My child seeks out arguments or reasons to become upset, even when everything is at peace. _____
9. My child ostracizes, scorns, and complains about others. _____
10. My child loses control when he or she is angry and shows it with facial expressions or body language. _____
11. My child uses foul language whenever he or she gets angry. _____

12. When my child is learning something new, he or she easily becomes frustrated and wants to do something else. _____

13. My child is stubborn and refuses to do what he or she is told to do unless you use the right tone of voice or approach. _____

14. My child's friends don't like to play with him or her because he or she is such a bad sport. _____

15. My child gets into fights with other children and has great difficulty controlling his or her temper when teased. _____

Total Score _____

Test Interpretation

0–5   Your child is remarkably free of anger and is not prone to frustration. If anything, he or she may be a little too passive—but don't try to change this!

6–10   Your child is showing a normal degree of anger and irritation, but the higher score (nearer 10) is more appropriate for younger children (under 6) and the lower score (nearer 6) more appropriate for older children.

11–15   Your child is beginning to show an above-normal degree of anger response. Again, the higher score is more appropriate for younger children. Some attention to your child's response may be needed.

16–20   Clearly your child has a problem with anger and should receive attention.

Over 20 Your child has a serious problem with anger, especially if he or she is already of school age. Take immediate steps to help your child cope with his or her anger, and seek professional help, if necessary.[3]

Dealing with Grief and Loss

Loss. It's a simple four-letter word. But what an impact it has on our lives. Do you remember the losses of your childhood? They were there, but perhaps you didn't always identify what you experienced as loss. Many children don't identify their losses as such, so they fail to grieve over their experiences. Some of the losses are obvious; others are not. Some are blatant, while others are subtle.

Life is a blending of loss and gain. Some losses are necessary for normal growth. For instance, a child discovers a tooth that is starting to wiggle loose. Soon it either falls out or is pulled. But the child learns that this loss is necessary to make room for the permanent tooth. The child loses a baby tooth but gains a permanent tooth (and sometimes a little money under the pillow).

UNGRIEVED LOSSES CONTAMINATE ADULT LIFE

The way we learn to handle losses in childhood impacts our lives as adults. The losses of adult life may actually be compounded by some of the unresolved losses of our childhood.

These are brought into adult life like unwelcome baggage. The losses vary in their complexity and intensity. For instance, some children are never allowed or encouraged to grieve over the loss of their favorite pet. They are told, *Don't cry. It's just a cat*, or *We'll get you a new goldfish tomorrow.*

A move can be a major loss for a child. A friend saying, *I don't want to play with you anymore* is a loss. Not making the Little League team, or simply not getting to play can devastate a child. Not having a favorite dress available for a special day can be devastating for an adolescent girl. Not getting the part in a play can spoil an entire week for some kids. We need to see the losses through the eyes of the child.

Sometimes the loss is a case of unexplained withdrawal of involvement on the part of the parents. When Ken was a child, both of his parents were actively involved with him in all of his soccer, Little League, and school activities. But when he turned 11, they not only stopped attending his activities, but they didn't even ask him about them. No explanation was given; he couldn't understand it and ached inside for some response on their part. But it never came. This disappointment led to a fear that *everyone will end up doing this to me,* and consequently, a sense of caution and suspicion began to develop within him. It showed in his relationships as an adult.

More and more people enter adulthood with a sense of loss because they were children of divorce. *Newsweek* magazine estimated that 45 percent of all children will live with only one parent at some time before they turn 18. The results of studies on children of divorce indicate that the effects are more serious and long-lasting than many parents are willing to admit. Studies released in England in 1978 showed that children of divorce have a shorter life expectancy and experience more illness than other children.

These children tend to leave school sooner as well. In New York City, which has a very high adolescent suicide rate, two out of every three teenage suicides occur among teenagers whose parents are divorced. Many others carry a pattern of insecurity, depression, anxiety, and anger into their adult years because of the extent of loss they experienced.

In divorce, children experience a multitude of losses. These not only include the disruption of the family unit, but also the possible permanent loss of one of the parents, the home, neighborhood, school, friends, standard of living, family outings, family holidays, self-esteem, and the list goes on.

When a parent dies, there is a sense of closure to the relationship and an opportunity to say a final good-bye. Children go through a rather predictable period and sequence of mourning. But the mourning period after a divorce is open-ended. It comes and goes depending upon the involvement of the noncustodial parent. If the parent does not stay involved, the children wonder if Mom or Dad will ever come back. And if not, then why not? The children will question what they have done to cause this situation. They aren't sure if the loss is permanent or temporary. The occasional birthday card, the weekly phone call, and the all-too-infrequent visits and vacations keep the fantasy alive that the parent might return home.

We are hearing more and more about childhood physical and sexual abuse. This is a damaging loss that contaminates adulthood. It is demeaning, takes away the innocence of children, and violates their perception of adults. They often learn to suffer silently, having lost the love of a parent, their dreams, and their innocence. They've lost their childhood.

Another damaging loss is abandonment. It is true that some children are physically abandoned, but many more children are emotionally abandoned. Often kids don't know why they feel so alone and abandoned. Their parents never leave them alone and their physical needs are met. But their emotional needs are neglected. They lack nurturing, hugging, and emotional intimacy. The verbal affirmations they so desperately need are shrouded in silence. Soon they begin to think that something is wrong with them, and they carry this perception with them into adulthood. Teenagers are particularly vulnerable because they often seem to want to be left alone, causing parents to withdraw. But the truth is teens need constant reassurance of their parents' love and attention.

Time after time I have seen the ungrieved losses of childhood interfere with an adult's ability to respond normally to life and relationships.

WHY CHILDREN FAIL TO GRIEVE

Children are not nearly as equipped as adults to handle loss. Their thinking processes are immature and undeveloped. They have few experiences from which to draw, lack the vocabulary to describe their thoughts and feelings, and take things literally. For instance, if you tell your kids that you have *lost* someone close to you, they may assume the person will be found again.

THINGS THAT INTERRUPT A CHILD'S GRIEVING

It's important for us as parents to identify things that may inhibit our children's abilities to grieve the losses they experience. The following factors most often contribute to this problem:

- The parents have difficulty grieving past or current losses.
- The parents are unable to handle and accept their children's expressions of painful experiences.
- The children are worried about how the parents are handling the loss and attempts to protect them.
- The children are overly concerned with maintaining control and feeling secure and may feel frightened or threatened by the grief.
- The children do not have the security of a loving, caring environment.
- The parent does not caringly prod, stimulate, and encourage the children to grieve.
- In the case of a loved one's death, children may question their role in making it happen. Their misplaced guilt is further enhanced if they have ambivalent feelings toward the loved one.
- The family fails to acknowledge and discuss the reality of death or loss.[1]

STEPS TOWARD APPROPRIATE GRIEVING

Regardless of the type of loss children experience, the following steps are important in the grieving process:

- Children need to accept the loss, experience the pain, and express their sorrow.
- Children require assistance to identify and express the wide range of feelings they're experiencing.
- In the case of death, children need encouragement to remember and review their relationship with the loved one.
- Children need help in learning to relinquish and say good-bye to what they have lost.

Kids also respond differently to loss depending on their age and level of emotional maturity.

GRIEF IN EARLY CHILDHOOD

Grieving occurs even in very young infants. Young children between four months and two years of age express distress when responding to loss. At this stage, separation from Mom is a significant loss. If the separation is sudden, the child will express shock and protest. Prolonged separation creates despair and sadness. The child loses interest in objects and activities that are usually pleasurable. Unless a caring individual steps into the vacated role, the infant will become detached from everyone.

Children between two- and five-years-old may manifest their grief in a number of ways. Because they don't understand the significance of the loss, they may ask seemingly useless questions. They may appear bewildered and tend to regress in their behavior, becoming demanding and clinging. If what was lost is not returned, expressions of anger will become frequent. An adult may need to assist children toward acknowledging and expressing feelings of loss. Many people make the mistake of removing children from familiar surroundings following a family death or trauma. This further undermines their sense of security and heightens the anxiety.

In the case of death, children at this age are obsessed with thoughts of the lost loved one and overwhelmed by an intense sadness. They tend to idealize this person, dwelling on reviewing and remembering their lost relationship.

Children between the ages of three- and six-years-old engage in what is known as magical thinking. They believe that their own thoughts can influence people and events. For instance, a child who is upset about a parent taking a trip, may wish the car would have a flat tire so the parent wouldn't leave. When the parent is killed in a car crash caused by a blowout, the child feels responsible.

This is an age when fears increase. Children become aware of threatening events in the world around them. They're curious about bodily functions. When they experience the death of a loved one, kids may ask questions like: *Can he still eat? Can he go potty? Does he cry? Will he get out of the box and hug me again?*

At this age, children don't understand the permanency of death. For them, it's reversible. When a pet dies young children may act as if it is still alive by calling it, asking to feed it, or looking under a bed for it. These kids see people and animals as cartoon characters—able to survive anything. To them, death is merely a deep, temporary sleep. Parents often reinforce this misconception by telling them that the dead person is *resting* or *just didn't wake up.* Even some of the terminology used by funeral homes reinforces the denial of the permanency of death—for example, *the slumber room.*[2]

Young children are centered on themselves and often fail to take into account the viewpoints and beliefs of others. They engage in their own private language, often talking past each other. They're unable to distinguish between themselves as the speaker and someone else as the listener. They assume their words carry more meaning than they actually do and have little concern whether the listener understands or not. At this age, kids are quite literal and can easily be confused by statements like: *Don't pull my leg. That's a bunch of baloney. Keep your shirt on. Don't give up the ship,* or *Hang in there.* This begins to change at around seven years old.

Young children often make their own unique connections. They tend to group objects, events, and people together in a way that makes sense to them but to no one else. For example, Tom's grandfather had a stroke while at a baseball game with him. Now, Tom becomes anxious whenever he visits the neighborhood playground because it is adjacent to a baseball field. His parents, though, don't understand what's wrong with him.

Children in this age-group often focus their attention on one detail of an experience and ignore everything else. They have difficulty seeing the whole picture clearly. They don't comprehend the significance of loss.

GRIEF IN PRIMARY CHILDHOOD

As children get older they develop the ability to understand loss and even death. They're especially vulnerable because they can grasp the significance of their losses, but have limited skills to cope with them.

When faced with loss, children may use denial as a coping mechanism. It's easier to act as if nothing has happened. Children also hide their feelings at this age because they don't want to look like a baby. Afraid of becoming out-of-control, children may vent their feelings only when alone. To others, they may appear insensitive, uncaring, and unaffected by the loss, leaving the parent unaware of the extent of their grief. At this age, children need to be encouraged again and again to vent their feelings. Allowing your children to see you grieve and talking about your own feelings can help them work through their grief.

In order to cope with the loss, these kids live in a fantasy world of their own making. In an effort to maintain the preexisting relationship with whatever or whoever they lost, these children engage in fantasy. They may tend to idealize the qualities of a lost loved one, and other members of the family don't fare as well when compared to their fantasies.

Five- through eight-year-olds can experience a variety of feelings ranging from misplaced guilt to embarrassment about being in some way different from their peers. They often feel pressure to be strong and self-reliant, brought on by their fear for themselves and concern for other family members. They may become more helpful than usual in order to shut out the pain of their loss and feel more in control.

GRIEF IN MIDDLER CHILDREN

Children between the ages of seven and twelve years old experience dramatic changes in their thinking processes. They develop conceptual thinking and problem-solving skills. They relate more to real-life people and events than to a fantasy or make-believe world. They begin to understand the meaning and ramifications of loss. If the loss is a death, they are now able to reflect on the consequences of death, and that's evident in their questions. They may ask: *What will happen to Frieda now? Who will take care of her grandfather? Will Bill have to move now?* Even though their thinking is more developed, they jump to conclusions. They don't always understand what they hear, especially if it is communicated to them in adult terminology. Adults need to communicate clearly to this child, using simple statements, repeating and rephrasing important points of the message.[3]

These kids are becoming more independent, but they are still fragile. In fact, they may exhibit some of the same responses as their younger counterparts. They struggle with feelings of helplessness and childishness but don't want others to know, so they often put up a facade of coping with their losses. They recognize the finality and irreversibility of losing someone or something they love, but still have difficulty accepting the reality of their losses. Thus, grief remains unresolved.

One of the main reasons children at this age have difficulty grieving—or often become stuck in their grief—is because parents are not always honest with them about losses. They attempt to shield their kids from pain and do not encourage them to grieve or teach them how to grieve. If parents shield their children from a loss, especially a family loss, their emotional development will be stunted. They must be included when the family grieves.

It's also important for us to understand the way children grieve. Children don't have an adult's capacity to tolerate intense pain for a long period of time. They are more likely to grieve intermittently; mourning the loss for a while, playing a short time, then returning to the grief. If children experience the loss of a parent at this age, they may mirror a symbolic behavior associated with that parent. Or, some kids may try to act grown up to mask their feelings of pain and helplessness. These kids are easy to spot—they become "little adults" who try to care for everyone else, or they act bossy and controlling. Given the right setting, these kids' fears can become phobias, and their physical concerns obsessive.

Most children at this age have limited opportunities to express their grief. Unfortunately, most of us have not been instructed in grief, so we tend to avoid those who are struggling with loss, or we end up making a lot of useless, inappropriate remarks. But our kids depend upon us as parents to help them work through their losses. They lack the developmental experiences that assure them that the pain of a loss will ease in time and go away. As parents, we need to encourage them to express their feelings as well as give them the confidence that they will survive the loss.

Given the right support and guidance, most of these kids will be able to handle and recover from both the minor and significant losses in their lives. In fact, the process can provide valuable learning experiences for them to grow on.

YOUR CHILD'S REACTION TO LOSS

The death of a loved one is an extremely difficult loss for all of us to handle. Within the last two years I've lost my 22-year-old son, an uncle, and two cousins. Grief is real and fresh for me. But for children, it's even more difficult because they lack the resources to handle such a serious loss. Let's consider the reactions of children to a serious loss such as death.

Fear

Children who experience the death of a loved one can experience a number of fears, including the following:
- Fear of losing the other parent, siblings, or grandparents—they tend to see the remaining people as candidates for death.

- Fear of their own death—this is especially true if the child was younger than the sibling who died, and this child is approaching the age at which the sibling died.
- Fear of going to sleep because they equate sleep with death—even the prayer, "if I should die before I wake . . ." reinforces this misconception. Dreams and nightmares intensify the fear.
- Fear of separation because of the perceived insecurity of the home and family—they no longer feel safe and protected. They fear that just about anything could happen to them. And they're hesitant to talk about their feelings because it may upset other family members. One young girl told me, "When Daddy died, I wanted to talk to my mother about it. But I was afraid to because it made her cry, and I didn't want the others yelling at me 'cause I did that."

Guilt

The second feeling associated with grief is guilt. It's difficult to identify all of the sources of guilt, but there seem to be three main reasons kids experience guilt when loved ones die:

1. They died because I did something wrong. I misbehaved!
Kids have a knack for remembering things they've done that they think were wrong. They may have made a mistake, broken something, or forgotten to say or do something. Just like adults, children can end up with an incredible list of *if only's* or regrets.

2. I wanted them dead. I thought it and it happened.
It's important to remember that young children believe they can actually make things happen by thinking them. It's easy for kids to think their anger or aggression killed the loved one. Because they take on this responsibility, they live in fear of being found out and punished.

3. I didn't love them enough.
It's common for children to believe that if you love someone enough, it will keep them from dying. They long for a second chance to make things right.

Anger

Another common grief response is anger. A number of beliefs trigger children's anger. They often feel abandoned and
left to face life on their own. They're angry because their
future has been dramatically changed — they won't be with that
special person anymore. They feel victimized by events that
are out of their control.

Kids may express this anger in different ways. It may be
targeted like a well-aimed bullet or sprayed in all directions
like a shotgun pellet. It may be directed at family members,
friends, teachers, pets, or even at God. It may be expressed in
tantrums, fights, silent hostility, or verbal blasts. As difficult as
it may be to experience these demonstrative expressions of
anger, it is a healthy sign. The alternative response — bottling
up this anger — can result in digestive problems and depression.

Confusion

Worth mentioning here is the sense of confusion that can
accompany the loss of a loved one. Just imagine that you are a
six-year-old child who has been raised in a Christian home
and your mother dies. You will probably wonder *Where is God?
Why didn't He keep my mother alive? Why didn't He make her well?
My uncle told me Mom went to be with God. Why'd He do that?* Not
only are children confused about God, but they are dealing
with a mixture of feelings about the person who died.

And they're trying to sort through the conflicting messages
and advice they receive from grown-ups. The expectations of
adults often create confusion. One adult may be implying, *Oh,
you poor little child. You must feel so sad and alone.* At the same
time, someone else may be giving the message that *Now you're
the man in the family. You'll have to be strong.* The child can be
confused by these conflicting messages that say be strong, sad,
in control, help others, let others help, and so on.

The child's memories of the deceased can also cause confusion. The survivors are talking about this person in a way that
conflicts with the child's memories. They are praising and

lauding her perfect qualities in a way the child cannot understand. The child may wonder, *Was Mom really as perfect as they say? I didn't know that. Sometimes I didn't even like her, and I thought she was bad when she yelled and went on and on. Maybe I was wrong. I hope no one finds out what I think.* You can see how this would create confusion as well as guilt for the child.

The mood fluctuations of others also generate confusion. Individuals around the child may be cheerful one moment and moody and quiet the next. While this is a normal response, the child is seeking stability and assurance from these people, and their changing moods cause her to question her own responses. She may ask herself, *Is it me? Did I do something wrong? Do they want me around or not?*[4]

HELPING OUR CHILDREN HANDLE LOSS

How can we help our children learn to handle the losses of life? Start early. Overprotection and denial robs our kids of the opportunity to develop the skills they'll need throughout their lives.

1. Give your kids permission to grieve and encourage them to talk and ask questions.

Whether the loss is the death of a family member, a major move, or the loss of a pet, your children need permission to mourn. For certain kids, permission may not be enough. Some kids need an invitation to share their feelings, but they also need to be taught how to express sorrow. A few sensitive, well-directed questions can help draw them out. If your children still cannot talk, don't force it. Just let them know that you are available and ready to listen when they want to talk. And you may wish to look for other ways for them to express what they're feeling.

Once your children begin to talk about their feelings, it may seem like you've untapped a gusher. They are, in their limited capacity, attempting to make sense of what has happened and regain their security. Children whose questions are answered, who are given a forum for discussion, have less need to fantasize and are much easier to help than nonexpressive children.

If your children don't share their feelings, watch for indirect questions or statements of concern and try to put their feelings into words for them.[5]

2. Be available when your children are ready to grieve.

Being available may be the most important element in helping your children grieve. Remember, they need affection and a sense of security. Touching them and making eye contact will provide comfort and reassurance. Let your kids know that it is normal to have ups and downs when grieving. They are not going crazy. Help them break the mourning into manageable pieces so they don't become overwhelmed. Using illustrations and word pictures can help them identify and talk about their feelings.

It may surprise you to find that your children will have the same range of emotions as you do. These emotions include anger, panic, numbness, sadness, and guilt. Children need their parents to help them identify their feelings, the source of those feelings, and express them in constructive ways. Following are some of the ways you can help them do this.

3. Give them opportunities for creative expression.

Children who have difficulty verbalizing their feelings may find it easier to express them on paper. Drawing is an effective way for kids to gain control over their emotional pain and eventually eliminate it. When the loss is a death, drawing is especially important because it allows kids to actually see what their feelings look like. That helps give them a sense of understanding and control.

Writing or journaling is also beneficial for children whose writing skills are developed. It's easier for kids to express on paper the reality of what's happened and their fantasies about it. Writing a letter to the deceased person or even to God can also be helpful. Encourage your children to read aloud and discuss what they've written. But remember to respect their privacy. The choice needs to be theirs.

4. Create opportunities for playtime.

Periodically, your children need to be encouraged to take a break from their grief and to play with friends. Play is an important type of expression for children, especially for younger children whose verbal skills are limited. In the safety of play, a child can vent various feelings. Play helps them regain a feeling of safety and security. It gives them a feeling of power over the effects of loss and allows them to separate themselves from what has happened.[6]

They may feel like they're betraying the deceased if they have fun or allow themselves some enjoyment. But play is a normal and beneficial part of their lives and gives them time to recuperate. It also helps them realize that life goes on.

5. Watch your expectations.

We need to be careful not to overprotect our children. Lecturing or making decisions for them is not helpful while they're coping with a loss. When possible, it is better if they learn to make their own choices and be allowed to grow through the experiences of their lives.

The flip side of this issue, though, is that adults often have expectations that are inappropriate for their children's age level. I've overheard parents or other relatives say, "You're going to have to take over now and be the man of the family (or be the strong one)." This is an unrealistic expectation and places too much of a burden on the child. These kinds of messages will short-circuit the child's grieving process. So be careful to give them age-appropriate responsibilities.

6. Dismiss their myths.

It's important to discover if your children are practicing magical thinking. Younger children are particularly vulnerable to this. For instance, your child may have argued with a friend and three hours later, the friend was killed in a car accident. Your child may feel responsible. One young girl told her dog to drop dead and the next morning it was dead. She thought she made it happen. Children tend to feel they cause things to happen with their thoughts. It's important to identify and correct these myths as soon as possible.

Kids will often be impatient with themselves because they feel sad longer than they think they should. They also feel that no one has ever felt the way they do, so they may be uncomfortable with their friends. They need to be told not to expect too much of themselves or others at this time, and encouraged to talk with their friends — especially those who have experienced similar losses.

7. Make honesty a policy.

While grieving, our children look to us for hope and encouragement. When they ask us questions, we need to avoid giving them platitudes, and instead, let them know it's all right to question *why* when bad things happen. We need to admit to them that we don't have all the answers, but that we'll get through it together. One mother told her six-year-old, "I know it is a sad time for you. We are all sad and wish things were different. There are many changes happening right now, but in time things will settle down. Someday the pain will go away. It may go away gradually and keep returning again and again, but as we help and love one another, it is going to go away."[7]

When you experience the death of a family member or friend, ask yourself if this is your child's first experience with death. If it is, your child will need your help to understand the loss and sort out his or her feelings about it. Be especially sensitive to the child's reactions and anticipate the unexpected. Use words and phrases the child can easily understand. It may help to rehearse what you plan to say with someone else first.

Always be clear and as factual as possible, telling the truth about the death and what caused it. When kids ask questions, give them accurate information such as, *Your brother's heart stopped beating and that is why he died.* It is better to use proper death language such as *Grandpa died,* rather than, *Grandpa passed away.* But be sensitive about how many details you give since some children may not be able to handle them. When you have no answer to their questions, say so. Let them know, though, that when you do, you will share it with them.

In her book *Helping a Child Understand Death,* author Linda Volga suggests that when parents are questioned about death, they tell their children something like this:

> We miss Grandpa, but we can be glad Grandpa doesn't hurt or
> feel sad anymore. His body is in the ground, but all that loved and

was loved by Grandpa is with God and we believe God will love him and care for him in a way more beautiful and wonderful than we can imagine. When people say Grandpa is in heaven, this is what they mean.[8]

Give your kids the option of attending the funeral. It helps if they're included in the rituals of saying good-bye. Viewing the body and being at the memorial and graveside service will raise a few questions while answering others.

8. Allow your children to respond in their own ways.

Don't expect your kids to respond as you do. Initially, they may not seem upset or sad. Young children may even have difficulty remembering the deceased. You may need to help them remember their relationship with the deceased before they can resolve their grief. Photos and videos may be helpful. Reminiscing about times spent together and reviewing certain qualities of the person may also be helpful.

Children often regress because they don't know how to grieve.[9] The important thing is to allow children to progress at their own rates. Just be available, or have someone else available, to observe their reactions. If they begin to express strong feelings, don't block them. Allow them to cry or express anger or even bitterness. In time, they will probably begin to ask questions. Answer them simply and honestly, even though you may struggle with them yourself.

9. Watch your kids for signs of fear.

Your children need reassurance that their family still exists, and that they are important parts of it. Children will tend to ask the same questions over and over again. Their questioning may become intense as they attempt to assimilate what has happened and how it will affect their lives. You may need an abundance of patience to answer them again and again in a loving way.[10]

Children may become especially aware of their vulnerability to losing other important people or things as they evaluate how this loss will affect their lives. Anything of importance to them could become the object of fear. It could be their home, school, friends, church, pets, a daily routine, an activity, or another loved one. They will require constant and consistent reassurance. And it's important to tell kids that, if there are any planned changes in the future, they will be discussed with them in advance.

10. Encourage children to continue normal routines.

It helps if kids continue certain family routines. Routines provide security and let kids know there are certain constants in their lives—things they can rely on to stay the same.

One of the most practical things parents can do is to encourage their children to take good care of themselves—to get plenty of rest and exercise, and to eat a balanced diet.

Loss is a natural and inevitable part of life. A key element in your children's emotional development is learning to deal with the feelings associated with loss and growing through the experience. Parents who guide their kids through the troubled waters of the grieving process will equip them to handle the losses of their adult lives.

7

Dealing with Fear
and Anxiety

Six-year-old Jimmy sat in the backseat of the car, stubbornly refusing to get out. His mother had ahold of his hand and kept telling him, "Jimmy, get out of the car now!"

"No," Jimmy said, "I'm scared. I don't want to go in there."

"Jimmy, now!" his mother replied sternly. "Get out of the car. You're not afraid. There's nothing to be afraid of. You're a big boy and too old to be afraid!"

Sound familiar? Jimmy was returning to the allergist who was going to stick him with those sharp pins again. It was a normal response for him to not want to go back. The problem here is the messages his mother is sending. She's denying his fear as well as subtly teaching him to not share his fears with others. Children will be afraid. And the fears they have cover a wide range of concerns.

WHAT IS FEAR?

Where does fear come from? Do children learn to be afraid or is it innate?

Our English word *fear* comes from the Old English *faer*,

meaning sudden calamity or danger. But it has come to mean the emotional response to real or imagined danger. The Hebrew word for fear can also be translated *dread,* a heavy, oppressive sensation of fear. A word we often interchange with fear is *anxiety,* which comes from the Latin *anxius.* To be anxious is to be troubled in mind about some uncertain event. A variation of *anxius* means to press tightly or to strangle. Anxiety is often a suffocating experience.

Fear and anxiety are actually quite similar. A true fear has an identifiable object of danger, either real (a burglar in the house) or imagined (a shadow that looks like a burglar). When we're anxious, we have the same feeling of fear, but we don't know why. The danger is subconscious.

Our language is rich in terms that describe fear, anxiety, and related emotional responses. Timidity describes a perpetual tendency toward fear, and panic is a sudden upsurge of terror. Consider other terms in the vocabulary of fear. Which of these best describes your children's feelings when fear strikes?

apprehension	horror	anguish
worry	concern	edginess
wary	upset	agitation
trepidation	dread	alarm
uneasiness	disquiet	misgiving
jitteriness	unnerved	aghast
perturbation	scared	terror
panic	nervousness	solicitude
qualm	sensitivity	unsettled
distress	consternation	fright

Fear is a protective response. It helps us adapt and adjust to potential danger. It keeps us alive and well. Children learn through experience what they need to fear. They need to anticipate the danger of certain situations, such as fire and other things that can burn, sharp objects, unsafe structures, or a pet that is being mistreated. Actually, the list is endless. Kids respond in different ways to danger. Given the same circumstances, one child perceives a threat and another of the same age does not. It depends on several factors, but underreacting to potential danger can be as harmful as overreacting.

DIFFERENT RESPONSES RELATING TO GENDER

There seems to be a difference between boys and girls when it comes to who might be the most fearful. Most studies indicate that girls report having a greater number of fears as well as more intense fears than boys.[1] Some have explained this as innate, just a gender difference. But it's more likely that experiences and environment have a lot to do with the differences. Our society has determined that boys and girls should respond quite differently to fear. Early on, these patterns are learned from parents, teachers, siblings, friends, and television.[2]

Girls are given more freedom and encouragement to admit to being afraid and to express their fears. Parents tend to be more cautious and restrictive with their daughters than their sons. And when daughters express their fears, they're likely to gain more support and comfort than a son would.

Boys are encouraged to be more masculine and courageous. Fathers tend to be upset when their sons show fear, and they often act quickly to put a damper on the expression of it. Unfortunately, if a boy cannot express his fear directly, it may come out in stuttering, depression, asthma, or sleep disorders.

FEAR AT DIFFERENT STAGES OF DEVELOPMENT

Children's fears change as they grow older. That's because their experiences change, as evidenced by the isolated life of the newborn and the exploratory behavior of the active two-year-old. As kids grow older their thinking, reasoning, and vocabulary abilities expand—and so does their potential for fear. The more they explore, the more cautions and warnings they receive, and the more hurts they experience firsthand.

Toddlers' fears are related to immediate situations. But preschoolers have a memory to draw from and may anticipate what could happen in the future. Life is scary for them, but much of this fear is in their imaginations. Two- to four-year-old children's most common fears are of the dark, being alone, and imaginary creatures. My co-author, Gary, told me about the reaction his two boys had when they saw the movie *Jaws* at ages nine and six. It was too real to them. Last year I saw the Disney film *Fantasia* for the first time since I was a child. All I remembered was enjoying it when I was young. I loved the animation and music, but I could see how scary some of the sequences might be for very young children.

Newborns and toddlers feel secure with familiar things. It's the new, the strange, and the unexpected that can trigger a fear response. Perhaps you've seen the fear of strangers in the face of your infant. Whenever our pastor conducts an infant dedication or baptism, I watch the expression on the child's face. At times when the parents are handing the child to Dr. Ogilvie, a look of wide-eyed stark terror comes over the infant's face. It's just a normal response for children of this age.

After about six months of age, most children begin to develop a fear commonly referred to as *separation distress*.[3] When children are alone but know Mom is somewhere around, they are comfortable. But when they can't find her, they may raise the roof with their cries. When they experience prolonged separation like hospitalization or abandonment, the fear and anxiety they experience can follow them throughout their lives. We've worked with numerous adults who struggle with the fear of abandonment. It usually developed in their childhood. Separation distress is one of those childhood fears that doesn't go away like so many others, but simply changes its form of expression.

As children move out of the infancy stage, two new manifestations emerge: a school phobia and a death phobia. We use the term *phobia* when describing an intense fear. All kids have some level of fear, but when they try every way possible to avoid something (like going to school), the fear may have become phobic.[4]

There are many fears children experience. Some of the most common are: animals and insects (children are more afraid of dogs than cats), the dark, death, doctors, dentists (I remember this one!), heights, dreams and nightmares, fantasy creatures, and especially monsters, school, storms, and deep water.[5]

Fears may take many forms and be expressed in several ways. As kids move through the school years, their fears are often individualized, depending on their own life experiences. Acts of violence portrayed on television or real-life tragedies or losses feed their fears. Some common fears which many kids experience relate to their social relationships and individual competence.[6] Children notice their differences and compare themselves to others. They are vulnerable to typical kids' responses of ridicule and rejection, and no matter what the age, it hurts. Did you ever experience the dread of being the last person chosen for the team? When the seeds of inferiority are planted, they tend to grow until the child's life is lived through the constancy of this fear.[7]

FEARS AND TEMPERAMENTS

Why are some kids more fearful than others? Are all fears learned or is there an inborn tendency to be fearful? Every child enters the world with certain predispositions. These personality characteristics are often referred to as temperaments. Even from birth there are some babies who are referred to as easy and some as difficult. We really don't fully understand why some kids are like this except that there is some evidence that genetics play a role, as well as the emotional state of the mother during pregnancy. Babies do tend to be affected by emotional and physical stress in the mother.[8] These are not just offhand opinions or labels but a determination based on the baby's responses to bathing, cuddling, feeding, and dressing.

But what's the difference? *Difficult* babies' patterns of eating, sleeping, and elimination are not regular or predictable from day-to-day as the *easy* babies' are. They don't adapt easily to new people or situations. Change throws them and fussing is usually the result. Crying is frequent and often without any identifiable cause. And it's not a quiet cry. It's usually wailing and screaming. Parents can become weary and frustrated since nothing they try works. These children tend to have a wider and more intense range of emotional responses. Because of this, a difficult child is more vulnerable to being fearful. Fortunately, only a small number of children fit this profile.[9]

FEAR IS LEARNED

Children are not born with fear. They learn to be fearful. It is developed; and therefore, it is preventable. How do kids develop fear? One way is through experience. One single traumatic event may be all it takes for that fear to gain a foothold and hang on for dear life. And if the upsetting experience is repeated several times, it can become much stronger. For instance, if a child eats a piece of fruit and becomes ill, she may have a fear of eating that fruit again. Another child may have had an accident while visiting the zoo. Now, every time his parents suggest visiting the zoo, he begins to feel fearful.

Years ago one of the girls in my high school group shared with me her experience with cats. As a young child, she was riding her tricycle around the block. Suddenly, a cat emerged from inside one of the houses, attacked her, and scratched her leg. After that, every time she saw a cat, or someone suggested getting her one, she became terrified. When I met her the fear was so intense that if someone brought a cat into the room, she would literally bolt out the door.

I had my tonsils taken out when I was six years old. My doctor told me I would be in the hospital for two or three days, and I could eat a lot of sherbet. But my adenoids bled for a week, and I had a very unpleasant experience. For years, whenever I would visit the doctor's office and smell the same hospital smells, I experienced a sense of anxiety.

When these fears are not dealt with, kids will generalize them to other situations or objects, and they can be carried into adult life. We've had parents ask us why their child is afraid of a specific item or situation. They're confused because the child has never been exposed to it or had a bad experience with it. Children's fears are often generalized to other things or experiences. A child who was attacked by a rooster while visiting a farm soon reacts with fear to most feathered animals, even stuffed animals. A child who locked herself in her closet soon refuses to go into any small room, and wants to leave the door open in both the bathroom and her bedroom. Another child, startled by a train whistle near his grandmother's home, fell off his bike. Since then, he jumps at any loud, piercing sound and often begins to cry. The next year, he threw a tantrum when his parents tried to take him on a train in an amusement park.

KIDS WHO ACQUIRE FEAR FROM THEIR PARENTS

How do kids learn to be afraid? They may actually learn some of their fears from us. Children learn through modeling or imitative learning. They like to imitate adults who are important to them. I may tell my child not to be afraid of going to the doctor, but if he sees me sitting in the waiting room—anxious, palms sweaty, thinking of ways to cancel the appointment—he will know that I am afraid.

When children are preschool age, they develop a finely tuned antennae that picks up fear in other people. This is an important skill because if helps them protect themselves when real danger exists. But the downside is that it gives kids another way to develop unnecessary fears. Kids respect and admire their parents. They see them as competent and strong problem-solvers who protect them from danger. When children see their parents fearful, they tend to adopt those fears and phobias as their own.[10]

One of the places kids observe fearful behavior is on television. TV is an extremely strong source of observational learning. It presents many unrealistic and exaggerated situations that tend to frighten children. It can actually initiate a fear of dangerous situations that are unlikely to ever happen to the child. If kids watch a lot of the mayhem portrayed on TV, they begin to believe that what they see is realistic, and that it could happen to them. Because of its emphasis on negative reporting, even newscasts fall into this category. Films like *The Birds* and *The Swarm* can create fears and phobias as well. But many of these problems can be overcome by parents watching and discussing the program with their kids. Unfortunately, parents often have no idea what their kids are watching.

THE POWER OF IMAGINATION

One of the greatest gifts we are born with is our imagination. We use it to create fantasies and daydreams. All of the world's best (and worst) ideas and inventions had their beginnings in someone's imagination. We can use our imagination in a positive or negative way. This ability to form mental pictures, including fearful ones, has tremendous power. A fearful image can sometimes interfere with reality. All of us are born with a sin nature, and unfortunately, it can affect a child's imagination at an early age.

Many kids between the ages of two and five years old have imaginary companions with whom they play and talk. They can't yet distinguish between what is real and what is imaginary. It's normal and appropriate behavior for them to even call on their imaginary friends to help them when they're afraid. But the same imagination children use to deal with fears can also create fears.

John was a boy with a number of fears. His mother couldn't come up with any reasons to explain why he had become so fearful. After several sessions of counseling, his therapist was able to discover that his fears came from some imagined events that John, with his limited abilities, thought were real.[11]

KIDS WHO LACK THE CONFIDENCE
TO HANDLE DANGER

Another source of fear in small children is that they feel helpless in the face of actual danger. As kids grow, they need to discover that they do have the ability to take care of themselves. Kids who lack this belief, or fail to receive encouragement to develop this confidence, are prone to being fearful. These kids can become fearful before anything actually happens.[12] They come to view themselves as weak and less capable or experienced. Fear begins to take over and eventually dominates their lives. Whenever children experience ongoing feelings of shame, anxiety, and inferiority, they may construct a vicious cycle which aggravates the problem. The fear soon becomes a self-fulfilling prophecy.

Ted is a nine-year-old who is very gifted at playing the piano. He lives with the fear of making a mistake while performing. At a recital last year, his fingers fumbled on the keys, causing him to lose his place. He was unable to finish the piece. To make matters worse, the same thing has happened twice since then. Now he lives with the constant dread of it happening again. His fear has grown so big in his mind that it actually affects his ability to perform.

Parents often ask me why their children's fears continue. We all tend to perpetuate our fears by inadvertently feeding them. For example, every time we avoid or run from something we fear, we give it power and control over us. If we as adults with our well-developed resources do this, imagine how easily our kids fall into this trap.

Many things influence a child's fears — temperament, experiences, thoughts, and imagination all play a part. For illustration sake, consider a hypothetical case created by Dr. Edward Sarafino. The boy's name is Alan, and he is afraid of birds. Imagine with me what this child's life would be like if all of the following conditions existed.

- He was born with a difficult temperament, making him less able to handle stressful events.
- His parents are impatient, frustrated, or infuriated when he reacts fearfully to birds.
- He later walks under a tree and birds swoop toward him, trying to protect their nest.
- He has a painful experience or suffers an injury that he relates to birds.
- He avoids birds (for instance, by staying indoors a lot).
- His fearfulness leads to secondary gains, such as not having to help with outdoor chores.
- His parents or friends are afraid of birds too.
- He sees birds attack people on TV or in the movies.
- He sees a horror movie that exaggerates the size and

power of birds (for instance, an enormous bird that devours a city).

- He sees a realistic film showing the predatory activities of eagles and pelicans and then thinks that he could become the victim.
- He is warned to stay away from a caged bird because it will bite him.
- He has nightmares about birds and thinks that these dreams are real events.
- He has no imaginary companion to rely on for emotional protection and support.
- He develops a negative self-concept and feels a sense of helplessness in stressful situations.[13]

Do you see why Alan might be fearful? Using fears your own children might be dealing with, ask yourself which conditions exist for them that may feed their fears. Keep in mind that whenever more than one of these conditions exists, your children's fears will compound and become exaggerated.[14]

PARENTS REWARD KIDS FOR SHOWING FEAR

Unfortunately, another way kids learn to fear is by being rewarded for their fear. Perhaps a parent allows children to get out of certain responsibilities or obligations because of fear. Or maybe they learn that they can get a lot of attention from parents and friends by appearing fearful. Some kids exaggerate their fear because of the attention they receive. I have seen kids walk into a yard with a small dog and be perfectly at ease when no adults are present. The same children with the same dog may behave much differently when adults are there to see their fear. They have been known to stop or start crying depending on whether or not a parent is watching. Parents can condition their children's fears by paying too much attention to their behavior.

RECOGNIZING YOUR CHILDREN'S FEARS

How do you recognize your children's fears? What are the indications that anxiety is present? Some children are very verbal about their fears, and you have little difficulty becoming aware of them. Others either avoid thinking about them or make it a point not to share their fears. But if children are quite fearful or troubled by anxiety, you might begin to notice some of the following symptoms emerging:

- difficulty concentrating;
- listlessness or hyperactivity;
- appetite changes—either eating very little or too much;
- bedwetting;
- nightmares;
- restlessness;
- insomnia;
- overly talkative or not talking at all;
- stuttering;
- panic attacks;
- compulsive behavior;
- obsessive patterns;
- physical complaints.

DEALING WITH FEAR OF ANIMALS

Let's look in more detail at some of these childhood fears and what can be done about them. For many children, an animal is an object of fear (for many adults as well). How do you help children who are afraid of an animal? First, realize that they lack the ability to cope with their fear all at once. So don't try to force them to face it suddenly.

Let's pretend the fear is of cats. Although cats look harmless, their claws are sharp. A cat may appear small to us, but think of it from a child's perspective. A 30-pound child sees a 15-pound cat differently than a grown-up does. Imagine a cat that is half of your weight and your response might be a bit more cautious. A cat can also bite and be unpredictable. Try the following approach when dealing with the fear of animals with your child.

Begin by gradually giving your child exposure to the animal. First, show your child pictures of a cat or point out certain qualities of cats on television or in a book. Let your child observe you enjoy handling a cat or looking at the picture of a cat. Let the child know he can pet the cat as you do. Don't force him, but when he does touch the cat, talk about how soft the cat's fur is, how pretty it is, etc. It is important to select a cat that is calm and responds positively to love and attention. Encourage your child to pet the cat with you more and more frequently. The time will come when he is able to do this on his own and be spontaneous about it.

Some parents have found it helpful to have their children keep a written record of their progress regarding whatever it is they fear. Such a written record shows kids they are attaining a goal. The record might indicate when they responded to a cat, how long, where, and their positive feelings.

DEALING WITH FEARS OF THE NIGHT

Our minds run wild during sleep. Darkness can be frightening, for it generates fears of being isolated, left alone, abandoned, or being lost. A gradual approach once again can be helpful with a child. Kids need to know that it is all right to talk about their fears, that we won't make fun of them for being fearful. You might try gradually reducing the amount of light in their rooms at night. Share with them Proverbs 3:24-26, and help them commit it to memory.

> When you lie down you shall not be afraid; yes, you shall lie down and your sleep shall be sweet. Be not afraid of sudden terror and panic, nor of the stormy blast or the storm and ruin of the wicked when it comes (for you will be guiltless). For the Lord shall be your confidence, firm and strong and shall keep your foot from being caught (in a trap or hidden danger). (AMP)

If your children struggle with nighttime fears, here are some ways you can help them overcome them.

1. Let your children know that it's all right to be afraid.

Everyone has fears at some time in their lives. A certain amount of fear is normal, and we don't have to be ashamed when we are afraid. By doing this you can reduce your children's feelings of guilt and shame. Share your own childhood fears, and let your children know that those fears passed from your life. This can be an encouragement to them.

2. Help your children understand that being afraid is temporary.
They may even fear that they'll be afraid forever. Give them a message of hope for the future, that will in turn create an expectation of success.

3. Let your children know that it is perfectly all right to talk about their fear.
Sharing their fear helps them keep it in perspective. It helps if you know the extent of their fear in order to help them overcome any distortions they may have. Many parents have found it helpful if their children draw their feelings on paper, or act out their fantasies, or use puppets to talk out their fears.

Sometimes children are fearful, but they have difficulty articulating what it is they're afraid of. It may be because they're too upset or don't have the verbal skills to adequately express themselves. It's not productive to try forcing it out of them or shaming them into telling you. Your best bet is patience and observation. You may find it helpful to keep a log of the times your children are afraid. By comparisons you can discover a pattern that will help you identify the source of their fears. Counselors often use picture books, allowing kids to point to whatever they're afraid of. Or they can use dolls to act out the situation. You might also try the sentence completion approach. You make up a sentence but leave the ending unfinished so the child finishes it for you.[15]

4. Let your children know that it is also normal not to be afraid.
When kids can observe another person not being afraid in a situation that scares them, they get the message that it is possible not to be afraid.

5. Help your kids learn a new response or behavior to replace their fear response.
These are called counter behaviors or fear replacing behaviors. Encourage your kids to imagine themselves not being

afraid in a situation that would normally frighten them. Positive imageries are powerful substitutes. It is difficult to be fearful and angry at the same time. Anger can give them a greater feeling of control. Participating in a positive activity or favorite pastime during a fearful situation can eventually lessen the fear.

As with adults, so it is with kids—repeatedly facing our fears is the best method of overcoming them. We need to teach our kids to tap the creative powers of their God-given imaginations to visualize themselves handling their greatest fears.

PREPARING YOUR KIDS TO AVOID FEARFUL EXPERIENCES

If parents can anticipate some of the most obviously fearful situations in their children's lives and address them in advance, it gives their kids reassurance. For instance, many children are afraid of the first day of school, going away to camp, going to stay with a relative, going to the doctor or hospital, and so on. By telling your children where they are going, letting them know what to expect, and how to handle the situation, they will feel much more comfortable and less likely to use their imaginations in a negative, fearful manner.

As a child, I went to the hospital when I was six, and again at nine. I don't remember much about either experience except that one of these visits was an emergency. Some kids have to be rushed in while others have plenty of time to think about the experience. You may think your child has no concern over the upcoming event because the child appears nonchalant and tells you that it's no big deal. Let your child know that some concern or apprehension is normal, then share some of your own experiences, allowing them an opportunity to talk about their fears.

STEPS TO FEAR-PROOFING YOUR KIDS

Raymond was seven years old and had developed gum problems. His dentist recommended pulling several of his teeth. Raymond had only been to his dentist a few times for check-ups and cleaning. His parents didn't want him to develop fears associated with going to the dental office, so here's what they did to prepare him for the extractions.

1. Both his mother and father sat down and shared with him that this visit was going to be different. (Fortunately, his parents were not the kind who complained about their own visits and how much pain they had experienced at the hands of their dentists.) They told him they would both be there and described what the dentist would be doing. They told him he could ask any questions of them or of the dentist.

2. They shared some of their own experiences and portrayed a calm attitude for him.

3. They went to the dentist for an additional examination and x-rays. The nurse and dentist described the procedure and showed him some of the instruments. The dentist had Raymond pinch his own arm so he would understand what the Novocain would feel like. They described what his recovery would feel like and kept encouraging him to ask questions.

4. His parents talked with him about comments his friends made about the procedure, and helped him think through what he would say to them if they made negative comments.

Parents who take their child to the hospital for an operation should follow a similar procedure. Public libraries and bookstores are a gold mine of helpful materials, many written specifically for children.

THINGS TO AVOID

How can parents help their children overcome a fear? There are several steps you can take that will be helpful, but also a number of things to avoid.

1. The forced approach is not helpful.

Some parents believe that forcing their kids to face their fears is the best approach to take. Unfortunately, it tends to make the problem worse because your children's emotional response to the fear blocks the rationalization of logic or facts. A gradual desensitization process will work much better.

2. Shaming or ridiculing only further aggravates your children's fears.

Many parents who feel frustrated or perhaps embarrassed by their children's demonstration of fear in front of others, may respond by shaming or ridiculing them. They may compare their kids to others, communicating messages like, *Why can't you be a big boy like Fred? There's nothing to be afraid of. Rabbits are nice animals.* We have to see fear through our kids' eyes, even though we don't personally relate to the fear.

We've seen some parents actually punish their children for being afraid. They use demeaning terms against them such as *bad, immature,* and *baby.* They threaten their kids with isolation in their room or being sent away until they learn to act grown up and brave. This only compounds their fears because they now have to deal with the fear of abandonment as well. If this fear gains a foothold, it will follow them into adult life and pollute their relationships. Even schoolteachers can be guilty of reinforcing this problem by misinterpreting children's fears as misbehavior.

3. Overprotecting your children keeps them from growing emotionally and learning to deal with fears.

While shopping, I recently observed an exchange between a mother and child that made me cringe. It was characteristic of the way many parents tend to overprotect their children. This mother was giving her daughter instructions, directions, and advice—most of which was not necessary. She reminded me of a hovercraft, and the child was obviously smothered by her. Kids raised in this kind of environment tend to be helpless, dependent, and lack self-confidence. Some of them resign themselves to the situation and develop the attitude that says, *OK, if they want to shelter me and take care of me, let them. I'll let everyone else do things for me throughout my life.*

The flip side of this are parents who ignore their children's fears and concerns. One father told me, "He'll just grow out of it. If I give him any attention, it will just make things worse. He'll learn." But how can kids learn with their limited capacity unless they receive guidance from someone who is more knowledgeable?[16]

THINGS TO DO

Now that we've covered some of the most obvious mistakes to avoid, let's look at specific things parents can do to help their kids overcome their fears.

1. Desensitization.

One of the best ways to help your children overcome their fears is through the process of desensitization. Understandably, many kids develop a fear of animals. I have a large golden retriever. He is a happy, loving, and friendly dog. He loves children, but I've had to teach him to lie down and wait for kids to approach him. He's frightened several small children. Just imagine being three feet tall and watching a huge dog run toward you with his tail wagging frantically, and his tongue hanging out of a huge mouth with giant teeth. You would probably run and hide behind your mom too. An experience like this could trigger a crippling fear that would be generalized to other dogs and animals. This is where desensitization comes into play. It's a gradual process of facing fear through small, positive steps. The best way to begin overcoming a fear is to face it a little at a time, from a safe distance.

2. Scripture memorization.

Memorizing God's Word at an early age is a positive step toward eliminating fears. The phrase *Fear not* is used 366 times in the Bible. Help your child memorize all or part of the following passages: "Fear not: for I am with you; do not look around you in terror and be dismayed, for I am your God, I will strengthen and harden you; yes, I will help you; yes, I will hold you up and retain you with My victorious right hand of rightness and justice" (Isaiah 41:10, AMP). "You will guard him and keep him in perfect and constant peace whose mind is stayed on You, because he commits himself to You, leans on You and hopes confidently in You" (Isaiah 26:3, AMP). "But now thus says the Lord Who created you, O Jacob, and He Who formed You, O Israel: Fear not, for I have redeemed you — ransomed you by paying a price instead of leaving you captives; I have called you by your name, you are Mine. When you pass through the waters I will be with you, and through the rivers they shall not overwhelm you; when you walk through the fire you shall not be burned or scorched, nor shall the flame kindle upon you. For I am the Lord your God, the Holy One of Israel, your Savior; I give Egypt for your ransom, Ethiopia and Seba in exchange for your release" (Isaiah 43:1-3, AMP). "Casting the whole of your care—all your anxieties, all your worries, all your concerns, once and for all—on Him; for He cares for you affectionately, and cares about you watchfully" (1 Peter 5:7, AMP).

3. Visualization.

Visualization means helping your kids visualize themselves safe in situations that might normally frighten them. For instance, in the case of a small boy who has a fear of dogs, you might begin by looking at picture books that are about dogs or that feature a dog as the character in a story. You'll need to review these books in advance, making sure they don't contain elements that might provoke or reinforce your child's fear.

Stuffed toys can be a useful transition leading up to the next stage—your child encountering a small, docile dog. At first, it may be enough just to have the dog in the same room, or your child playing near a dog that cannot come in contact with him.

One mother kept a record of progress with her child. It looked something like this:

> **Monday:** Ken played in a room for a while with the dog in another room.
> **Tuesday:** The dog came into the same room and sat tied up for 15 minutes while Ken played.
> **Wednesday:** I petted the dog and played with it while Ken played with his toys. I mentioned that his mouth was opened and his tongue was out because he's smiling and happy.
> **Thursday:** I played with the dog and Kenny played on the other side of me.
> **Friday:** Kenny petted the dog and the dog wagged his tail each time. I showed Ken how happy the dog was when he petted him.
> **Saturday:** Ken petted the dog and played with him for a few minutes.

Sunday: Ken hugged the dog and played with him. He didn't seem to mind that the dog wiggled. He even touched some of his teeth and let the dog lick his fingers.

Monday: Ken played with the dog and we began talking about going to see a larger dog. He was open to the suggestion.

Keeping a log like this can help you plot the progress of your child.

4. Make a plan.

In reducing any fear like this it's important for you to think up several approaches. Actually, coming up with 15 or more steps is helpful even if you don't use them all. Try to determine which steps are the most and the least fearful. Each step you take to expose your children to their fears should be a bit more fear-arousing than the previous one. Keep the steps gradual in their progression, and as kids master each step, let them know how far they've come. They need to build on their successes.

Don't expect immediate improvement. It will take several sessions of exposure (anywhere from a few moments to as much as 30 minutes each), to reduce a moderate fear. Be sure your kids proceed at their own pace. Don't rush them. Try to end every encounter on a positive note. Begin each new encounter where they left off the day before. And above all, be flexible and willing to adapt and experiment.

Fear of the dark is a typical fear for many children. The following steps are effective in eliminating this fear.

Fear Hierarchy for Overcoming the Fear of the Dark

1. Your child is in a room sitting with a friend and the lighting is fairly dim.
2. You and your child light two candles, and you turn off all the electric lights.
3. You and your child are in the room together, and your child blows out one of the candles.
4. You and your child and a friend are in the room together. The friend blows out one candle and your child blows out

the remaining candle. You talk to each other while the room is dark. After five seconds your child turns on an electric light.

5. You and your child repeat step four, but this time you wait a full minute before turning on the light.

6. You and your child repeat step five, but this time you wait five minutes before turning on the light.

7. Your child is alone in the room and the electric lighting is dim.

8. Your child is alone in the room and there are only two candles lit.

9. Your child is alone in the room and there is only one candle lit.

10. Your child is alone in the room and there is only one candle lit. Your child calls a friend on the phone, blows out the candle, and talks for a couple of minutes. Then she turns on the electric light and finishes her phone conversation.

11. Your child is alone in the room, and there is one candle lit. She blows it out and waits five seconds before she turns on the electric light.

12. Your child repeats step 11, but this time she waits 20 seconds.

13. Your child repeats step 11, but this time she waits a full minute.

14. Your child repeats step 11, but this time she waits five full minutes.

The number of steps may vary depending on your child's needs. The more gradual the approach to the fear, the more steps you will want to include. Whatever fears your children may have, you can take the steps outlined for you here and structure a fear reduction plan designed for each specific fear.

KNOW WHEN TO SEEK PROFESSIONAL HELP

Parents wonder — When are my child's fears so intense that professional help is warranted? The following questions will help you evaluate the level of your child's fear:

- Does your child have an abundance of fears? Is he or she afraid of just about everything?
- Is there any fear that is intense enough to interfere with the entire family's functioning and activities?
- Do your child's fears interfere with any social relationships or schoolwork?
- Is your child an unhappy child in general?
- Do your child's fears drive others up the wall? For instance, some kids are afraid of bugs to the extent that they refuse to enter any room unless someone has checked it out. One child I know had to check the doors and windows every 15 minutes to make sure they were locked.
- Is your child fearful or worrisome but cannot let you know what is bothering him or her?
- Is there any chronic physical condition such as colitis, asthma, ulcers, hypertension, or headaches that seems to be triggered by emotional stress?
- Have any fears intensified or continued over the past year?
- Have you tried to help your child but with no success?
- Are there any major family difficulties such as abuse, drug or alcohol problems, marital problems, etc.?

A definite *yes* answer to one of these questions and a qualified *yes* to several others indicates that professional help may be a wise choice.[17]

8

Dealing with Guilt
and Shame

I was jogging when I heard a father yelling at his son.

"You are absolutely worthless. You can't do anything right."

I looked toward the sound of his voice and saw a large man, well over six feet tall, looking down at his son who was about seven or eight years old. I'll never forget the look on that little boy's face.

As I continued running, I experienced a rush of conflicting emotions. My most immediate response was that I felt like crying. I could feel the fear, hurt, pain, and rejection I saw etched on his little face. I sensed his feelings of failure and worthlessness. He tried to hold back the tears but couldn't. I couldn't hold mine back either.

Another part of me wanted to run up and grab that father, shake him, and ask him if he had the slightest idea what he was doing to his son. But he was bigger than me. Anyway, it wouldn't have helped. People who are controlled by their anger have difficulty hearing anyone.

Perhaps the little boy had made a mistake or done something wrong. Maybe he hadn't listened to his dad. Possibly he had taken something from the garage he wasn't supposed to. He might have deliberately done something he knew was wrong. He may have even made this mistake several times. But he didn't deserve this kind of treatment.

Can you relate to this story? Did it remind you of your own childhood memories, or perhaps a time you responded in anger to one of your children? What effect do you think this experience had on the little boy? If this was not an isolated interaction but rather typical of the way this father communicates with his son, what effect do you think it will have on the boy?

I kept running, but I couldn't shake this scene from my mind. It reminded me of a man I had worked with several years earlier. Ken had grown up in a Christian home. His father and mother were leaders in the church. As a child, he had accepted Christ as his Savior and grew up wanting to serve God. He had gone to college and then married. After college he went to seminary and eventually became the pastor of a growing church.

I met Ken when he attended my pastor's workshop. Following the session, he came up to the front to shake my hand and thank me for the helpful information. Then, he handed me a note and walked away. Several others were waiting to talk with me, so it wasn't until I got back to my office that I had a chance to read his note. It read:

Dear Dr. Oliver:
Today it has become clear to me that I need to talk with someone about some problems that I have never shared with anyone. They are hindering my effectiveness as a husband and father, and limiting what I know God wants to do through me as a pastor. I'd like to talk with you about them. I'll call you next week.

Ken

Ken was the middle child in his family. He had an older brother and a younger sister. His older brother was strong, muscular, athletic, handsome, popular, and did well in school. Ken wasn't like his older brother. He wasn't especially strong, he didn't have an athletic build, he was average-looking, he wasn't good at sports, and he struggled with his grades. Ken was a nice, average, normal, pleasant little boy. But that wasn't good enough.

Ken shared his feelings with me. "As I look back on my childhood, it's clear that enough was never enough. I was always compared to my older brother who could do everything but walk on water. Or else I was compared to my dad who at my age could do more than Superman himself. I remember my dad frequently saying, 'Why can't you be like your brother?' or 'You're so lazy, you stink.' "

Ken told the story of coming home from school one day with his best report card ever. "I was so excited. I kept looking out my bedroom window, waiting for Dad to come home so I could run downstairs and show him my grades." With tears in his eyes, he shared with me his father's response: "See, I knew you were lazy. You could have done this all along. From now on, all of your grades should be nothing but A's."

With a faltering voice Ken told me, "All my life I felt guilty because I wasn't good enough, smart enough, or athletic enough. I'm tired of beating myself up. I'm tired of feeling guilty for just being me."

I paused as he wiped a few tears from his eyes, then said, "Ken, what you've struggled with isn't guilt. You have spent your life struggling with an out-of-control emotional response to shame. Shame and guilt are similar, yet distinctly different." Ken's eyes sparked with curiosity as he asked me to tell him more.

Guilt and shame are God-given emotions that, when properly understood, have a positive, constructive effect on our lives. Misunderstood, they can destroy us, leaving us emotionally crippled as adults.

Many parents struggle with feelings like Ken has described, but with the best of intentions, are creating a similar environment in their own families. If we want to raise emotionally strong and healthy children, we must understand the role guilt and shame play in their development.

UNDERSTANDING GUILT

A story is told of a time when Sir Arthur Conan Doyle decided to play a practical joke on twelve of his friends. He sent them each a telegram that read: "Flee at once . . . all is discovered." Within twenty-four hours, all twelve had left the country.

Most of us don't feel quite that guilty, yet many people go through their entire lives struggling with the emotion of guilt. *Webster* defines guilt as the fact of having committed a breach of conduct, especially violating law and involving a penalty. A person who is guilty is justly chargeable with or responsible for a grave breach of conduct.

Guilt is a powerful emotion that, like other emotions, can have a positive or negative effect on our lives. It can warn us of danger and motivate us to take corrective action. It can rob us of our joy or open the door to greater joy. It can distort our perspective or help us see things from God's perspective. We can allow guilt to keep us imprisoned in our past or serve as motivation to learn and grow beyond our past.

Developmental psychologists have found that guilt in children cannot be experienced as an emotion before the age of four or five. It is not until then that children begin to internalize a socially accepted standard of behavior. Before that age, the bulk of their good behavior is motivated more by a fear of punishment and a desire for reward rather than by guilt feelings associated with breaking clearly understood rules. When children younger than this commit some impropriety, the feelings that follow are usually not of guilt but rather fear stimulated by the anticipated consequences of discovery.

Beginning around four or five years old, children begin to develop a basic sense of right and wrong, based primarily on what they've seen and heard from their parents. They strongly adhere to the belief that wrongdoers (including themselves) must be punished and should apologize and make restitution for their mistakes.[1]

Healthy guilt is caused by behavior. When we have done something that is wrong—when our behavior violates a certain standard—we experience guilt. It usually comes from several sources. The first is civil or legal guilt which involves a violation of society's laws. The second is spiritual guilt which involves a violation of God's clearly revealed laws. The third might be called relational guilt which involves a violation of mutually agreed-upon standards of behavior. Guilt resulting from these three sources is usually real and objective guilt.

Healthy guilt is constructive. It is an appropriate emotional response to the clear violation of a civil, spiritual, or relational standard. Healthy guilt is a gift from God. Guilt is to our spirit what pain is to our body. It warns us when something is wrong and needs attention or correction. As Christians, it's important to remember that God has given us a way to remove the painful feelings of guilt. In Leviticus 4–6 God gave the Israelites three specific steps they could take to resolve healthy guilt. First, confession (5:5), then restitution (6:1-5), and finally sacrifice (6:6-7). In Psalm 51:17 we read, "The sacrifices of God are a broken spirit; A broken and a contrite heart, O God, Thou wilt not despise." Healthy guilt leads to a contrite heart that produces positive change in behavior. This in turn results in a closer walk with our Lord.

But not all guilt is healthy. Unhealthy or destructive guilt is an emotional response that doesn't relate to wrongdoing. I have met many Christians who have spent most of their lives feeling guilty without knowing why.

A friend of mine worked as a group facilitator in an inpatient recovery facility for six months. One day her purse was stolen. She went around the group and asked if anyone in the group had taken the purse. One of the patients answered, "I didn't take the purse, but I feel like I did."

That's unhealthy guilt. Psychologists call it *free-floating* guilt. It isn't caused by anything we've done wrong, but is rather a result of dwelling on our failures, shortcomings, and general unworthiness. We aren't quite sure what we've done, but we know we must have done something. We believe that if we are miserable enough, God will know that we are sincere.

We've talked with Christians who believe that feeling guilty is a sign of spirituality. But true spirituality is not measured by how sad we are, nor how serious, nor the degree to which we make everyone around us miserable. That's not the fruit of the Spirit; it's the fruit of the adversary. The fruit of the Spirit is love, joy, peace, patience, kindness, goodness, faithfulness, gentleness, and self-control.

In some cases, unhealthy guilt stems from a very serious sin in the past. Although these individuals have asked forgiveness (perhaps hundreds of times), they don't feel forgiven and continue to function as if they are still under condemnation for that transgression.

Several years ago I worked with a Sunday School teacher who had faithfully studied the Bible and led others to the Lord, but whose life was characterized by an overwhelming sense of guilt. This stemmed from a sin she had committed several years earlier.

She had confessed her sin, repented, and made restitution to the best of her ability. Yet she still didn't believe she deserved to experience the joy of the Lord. She taught her Sunday School pupils that the blood of Jesus Christ cleanses us from all sin, but she hadn't applied that promise to her own life. She lived as though Christ's blood only cleansed certain sins.

At our first session, she poured out her heart and asked if I thought there was any hope. She was shocked when I gently said, "Lois, I believe that your response to your past sin may involve an even greater sin."

"How's that?" she asked.

"Well, I think it's possible that one of the sins in your response may be the sin of pride," I replied.

"What do you mean?" she asked. "I don't think I'm a prideful person." She was puzzled by my remark.

I went on to point out the fact that it takes an abnormally inflated view of self to believe that someone can commit a sin so great that God can't forgive it. When we focus on our failures, we are choosing to dwell on what we have done and ignore the reality of what He has done. The focus is no longer on Christ but on us.

The implications of a Christian wallowing in the guilt of sins that have been confessed are tremendous. To teach that Christ has died for our sins, and then live as though He hasn't, is a blatant contradiction. Christians who choose to stay stuck in the rut of perpetual penance do a great disservice to themselves, to those close to them, and to the cause of Christ. They limit God, quench the Holy Spirit, live lives inconsistent with the Gospel message, and actively drain and discourage those around them.

When we choose to be miserable over past mistakes that we have taken to the cross and that God has forgiven, we are saying to our children and those around us that the blood of Jesus Christ isn't adequate to pay for our sins.

After several sessions, the Lord helped Lois see Psalm 51:7 and 1 John 1:9 from a new perspective. She was able to cast off the yoke of her self-imposed subjective guilt, and her life became more consistent with her beliefs. For the first time in years, she began to experience the joy of having a new song in her heart (Psalm 40:1-3).

The result of this change was that she became less negative and critical. Her friends told her she seemed more positive and was more fun to be around. It became easier for her to compliment and encourage her children, her husband, and her friends.

In his *Letters to an American Lady*, C.S. Lewis gives a valuable insight on guilt:

> Remember what St. John says: "If our heart condemn us, God is stronger than our heart." The feeling of being, or not being forgiven and loved, is not what matters. One must come down to brass tacks. If there is a particular sin on your conscience, repent and confess it. If there isn't, tell the despondent devil not to be silly. You can't help hearing his voice (the odious inner radio) but you must treat it merely like a buzzing in your ears, or any other irrational nuisance.
>
> Remember the story in the Imitation, how the Christ on the crucifix suddenly spoke to the man who was so anxious about his salvation and said, "If you knew that all was well, what would you, today, do, or stop doing? When you have found the answer, do it or stop doing it." You see, one must always get back to the practical and definite. What the devil loves is that vague cloud of unspecified guilt feeling or unspecified virtue by which he lures us into despair or presumption. "Details, please?" is the answer.[2]

Unhealthy or destructive guilt causes you to focus on yourself and leads to discouragement, depression, a distorted perspective, and more guilt. Healthy guilt is a painful yet valuable emotion. It is important for us to model this emotion and help our children develop the ability to experience it, express it, and know how to deal with it. Healthy or constructive guilt draws you to Christ and leads to action that results in reconciliation, recovery, and renewal.

Healthy families are not full of perfect people. They are made up of people who are redeemed, who hunger and thirst after righteousness, who are in recovery, who are being restored, and people who have opened their lives to Christ's power and are becoming conformed to Him. The God-given emotion of guilt is an integral part of that process.

UNDERSTANDING SHAME

Whenever we are criticized, made fun of, or put down, we experience the emotion of shame. Whenever we do something in public that embarrasses us and causes people to laugh at us, we experience shame. Whenever our performance falls short of our expectations, we experience some degree of shame.

Shame is an emotion caused by the awareness of our shortcomings, improprieties, or guilt. It is a temporary emotion that can be caused by something as simple as making a mistake or saying something foolish. It can be experienced as merely uncomfortable or as massively painful. The intensity of the emotion varies with the situation.

While guilt and shame are related, there are important differences that we need to understand. Healthy guilt comes from doing something wrong, or not doing the right thing. Healthy shame alerts us to the fact that we have fallen short. It makes us aware of legitimate guilt. It motivates us to examine our behavior, confess our sin, make amends, learn from the experience, and move on.

Shame tells us that we are fallen, flawed, and finite. In itself, that's not bad. All of us are in some way flawed. We all have strengths and weaknesses. Romans 3:23 tells us that "All have sinned and come short of the glory of God." As we are able to identify our blind spots and weaknesses, we can work on those particular areas. God can help us develop creative alternatives.

Experiencing the emotion of shame is a universal experience. In many ways, it can be a comforting experience. We are all sinners, we are all unworthy, we are not alone in our flaws and vulnerabilities, and we are all equal in God's eyes.

Shame becomes crippling when we believe that we are, at our very core, worthless human beings. Once we allow shame to define who we are, once shame becomes the basis of our identity, it becomes dehumanizing and toxic.[3]

Toxic shame gives us a sense of terminal worthlessness. It says that our basic nature, our core identity, is inadequate and unlovable, and always will be. We tell ourselves that, *This is who we are and we will never be different. We will always be this way. And once people find out what we are really like, we won't have any friends.*

What's the difference between healthy guilt and toxic shame? Guilt says *I did wrong,* shame says *I am wrong.* Guilt says *I made a mistake,* shame says *I am a mistake.* Guilt says *I failed,* shame says *I am a failure.* Guilt says *I did something bad,* shame says *I am a bad person.*

Toxic shame is frequently instilled at a young age as the child internalizes a parent's contemptuous voice, ostracism, sarcasm, rebuke, teasing, or ridicule. Sometimes, what becomes shame started out as blame. *It's all your fault. If only you could get your act together, we wouldn't have these problems!* It's very easy for a family to blame all of its problems on one member.

The blame becomes shame when fault-finding remarks turn into constant put-downs. *You're no good. You always do the wrong thing. You'll never amount to anything!* The family ends up attacking the child's basic identity.

Toxic shame causes people to become inordinately self-conscious. When we forget who we are in Christ and become focused on our fears, flaws, failures, and limitations, it's hard to see anything else. It's similar to what happened to the Jews at Kadesh-Barnea. As they focused on their circumstances and limitations, they became "like grasshoppers in our own sight, and so we were in their sight" (Numbers 13:33, NASB).

Toxic shame can silence us. Because of our fear of saying or doing the wrong thing, because of our fear of looking stupid and being ridiculed, we don't say or do anything at all.

Toxic shame can keep us from trusting others and developing close, intimate relationships. Since we see ourselves as terminally worthless, it follows that if others see us as we really are, they will reject us. Rather than face the possibility of the painful humiliation of rejection, we keep a wall around us so that no one will ever see the real person.

Toxic shame can render us powerless. Since we are afraid of failure, we become reactive rather than proactive. Instead of seeking God's direction for our lives and moving out in a proactive sense of confidence, we simply react to life. We spend our time reading our environment and trying to figure out what is expected of us, and how we need to respond to staying out of trouble and gaining others' approval. Toxic shame keeps us from becoming the unique men or women that God designed us to be.

Over time, toxic shame can cause our lives to be characterized by remorse, self-hatred, jealousy, bitterness, resentment, hopelessness, helplessness, hurt, frustration, depression, low self-esteem, and irrational fears. We tend to be accident prone, seeking punishment for our many flaws. We respond by lying and stealing, and may resort to physical violence.

When we are shamed, our immediate impulse is to cover up, hide, and divert attention from ourselves, presenting only a false image of ourselves to the world. In fact, the etymological root of the word *shame* means *to cover*. We begin to believe that we are hopeless and helpless; therefore, our only hope is to develop a false self. We try to make people believe we are someone other than who we really are. That *someone else* is often whoever we think others expect us to be.

As children, we tend to develop in ways that fit in with our environment. If our home is characterized by openness, honesty, flexibility, and unconditional love, we are free to grow in the unique ways that God designed us. We are free to be the same as, or different from others in our family. If our home is characterized by rigidity, negativity, and conditional love, we will tend to act in ways that don't threaten or make waves. Rather than discover who we are in Christ, we substitute our true self for a false self who is more acceptable to our parents, whose love and approval we desperately need. We exchange the image of God for the image of our parents' insecurities, inferiorities, and toxic shame.[4]

Some of us respond to toxic shame by developing a narcissistic, false self. We may seek to perform in ways that draw attention to ourselves. We may seek out individuals who constantly tell us how great we are, and turn away from anyone who does not frequently acknowledge how wonderful we really are. Narcissism is associated with inordinate self-adoration, grandiosity, and an annoying attitude of entitlement. Yet, over the years, I've been surprised by the number of narcissistic individuals I've worked with whose problems stem from an unhealthy sense of shame.

Other people respond to toxic shame by trying harder. They become overachieving and perfectionistic workaholics. Eventually, they will find themselves in a constant state of dissatisfaction. Any imperfection is exaggerated and viewed as a deformity. Children raised in perfectionistic homes internalize these values from their parents. They don't have the mental capacity to distinguish whether their parents' values and standards are good or bad, right or wrong, healthy or unhealthy. In childhood, we acquire morals, values, and ways of responding that become a part of who we become as adults. They operate on a preconscious level and are manifested as automatic responses.

When children grow up with a shameful self-concept, certain aspects of their lives can be governed by these distorted perspectives:

> A boy who is ashamed of being needy may become a caricature of independence, unable to ask for help or closeness or even to feel those longings within himself without risking the disintegration of his self-regard. A girl who feels unloved by her mother may grow up with a nagging sense of shame about wanting and valuing others more than they want or value her and may establish relationships in which she is never the seeker, always the sought. A woman who secretly despises herself for being selfish may feel that she should not take, should not ask, should not calculate in her own behalf, and she may compensate for what she sees as her shameful self-seeking with rigid displays of generosity. No one must ever see that clawlike third hand reaching out of her pocket with "Selfish!" written all over it.[5]

NOW THAT I UNDERSTAND THE BASICS, WHAT CAN I DO ABOUT IT?

1. Ask God to help you be aware of your own issues. Many parents shame their children because of their own unidentified and unresolved issues. Because they were never accepted for who they are, they may have a difficult time accepting their kids for who they are. They may want them to be bigger, stronger, quicker, smarter, prettier, bouncier, more aggressive, more compliant, and more or less of any number of characteristics.

2. Ask God to help you appreciate the uniqueness of each one of your children and to be aware of their real needs.

3. On a daily basis, tell your children that you love them. Nothing defends against the attacks of toxic shame like the security a child receives from the love and acceptance of his or her parents. When your children know that you love and appreciate them for who they are, and when they know that you respect their feelings, differences, and peculiarities, they are free to grow into the unique people God intended them to become.

4. Affirm your children several times a day. Let them know that they are of infinite worth and value and are precious to you. In 1 Corinthians 13:7 we read that love "bears all things, believes all things, hopes all things, and endures all things." At times this will be easier said than done, especially if you try to do it in your own strength. But the Bible commands us to love one another, build up one another, nourish one another, cherish one another, and encourage one another. Each week pick one of the *one anothers* and ask God for creative ways to model it for each of your kids.

5. Give them quality time. This can be especially powerful after they have made a mistake or done something wrong. Intentionally spending time with them lets them know that your love is, like Christ's love, unconditional. This tells them that even when they make mistakes, they are significant, they are of infinite value and worth.

6. Listen for your kids' statements of guilt and shame. Let

them talk themselves out. Help them differentiate between the healthy guilt that comes from wrong behavior
and the unhealthy shame that can damage their identities.
They need to know that they can share whatever they
have done, thought, or felt without threat of being
rejected.

7. Don't use guilt-inducing techniques as a way to get them
   to do what you want. Making fun of your children or
   attempting to shame them out of their emotions is an
   unhealthy and destructive practice. We can demoralize
   them when we communicate messages like, *Why are you
   crying? I can't believe you're being such a baby about this. All the
   other kids are having a good time. Why are you being so difficult?* or *Jeff isn't afraid. What makes you such a scaredy-cat?*
   Shaming is humiliating and makes kids feel doubtful, inferior, and inadequate. It doesn't cause them to respond
   positively or make them feel better.[6]

8. Be quick to forgive your children. Sometimes it is easy for
   parents to hold a grudge against their kids, especially if
   something their kids have done has made them look bad
   in the eyes of others. If you are a parent, you know exactly
   what I'm talking about.

9. Be aware of your verbal and nonverbal communication.
   I've read many books that talk about the damaging effects
   of physical punishment. But, in an effort to influence and
   control their children's behavior, some parents withdraw
   their love, attention, approval, and affection. They speak
   to their kids in a sarcastic and demeaning tone of voice.
   They have moved from physically punishing them to de-
   grading and humiliating them.

10. Remember that you are dealing with children. The youn-
    ger your children are, the more limited their capacity to
    understand abstract concepts like emotions. However,
    their emotions are very real and valid to them. They don't
    understand them but they know when they feel good or
    they feel bad. Remember to affirm their feelings—whatev-
    er they are. There are no right or wrong emotions. Chil-
    dren can't always help what they feel, nor can they change
    their emotions on command.

WHAT HAPPENED TO KEN?

Do you remember Ken, the pastor from the beginning of this chapter? Well, over a period of several months, Ken and I discussed many of the principles shared in this chapter. As he reflected on his childhood, he saw that his dad had good intentions. He meant to give constructive criticism. He wanted to motivate his son to lose weight, watch less TV, and study harder. However, his dad's constant criticism became blame, which had a shaming effect on Ken.

Ken responded in two different ways. At first he responded by giving up. He medicated his pain by developing close relationships with his two best friends — the refrigerator and the TV. Whenever he felt bad (which was most of the time) he ate. He also found that it was much easier not to think and feel when his mind was occupied, so he became addicted to television.

When we implement the principles of redemption in our family relationships as well as our own lives, we can overcome the tendency to model unhealthy guilt and shame. By becoming partners with God in our parenting, we can teach our children healthy responses to the powerful emotions of guilt and shame that will help them develop a more intimate relationship with their Creator.

9

Identifying Stress in Your Children

Stress is no respecter of age, gender, educational level, profession, or social status. We are all susceptible to experiencing the effects of stress in our everyday lives. As one ten-year-old described, "I feel like a rubber band that someone has twisted again and again, and I'm all wound up." This child was experiencing stress.

It's not uncommon for even newborn babies to suffer from stress. Medical research has determined that mothers who experience extreme turmoil during their pregnancy often give birth to babies with peptic ulcers. Stressed children are more apt to struggle with and express a wider range of emotions than calm children.

WHAT IS STRESS?

Stress is any life situation that chronically bothers, irritates, or upsets you, your child, or your family. It can be any type of situation that places conflicting or heavy demands on your body. Stress demands upset the body's chemistry and equilibrium.

HEALTHY AND UNHEALTHY STRESS

Your children's bodies come equipped with a highly sophisticated defense system that helps them cope with threatening or challenging events in life. When they feel pressured or threatened, their bodies quickly mobilize their defenses for fight or flight. In the case of stress, an abundance of adrenaline pumps through their bodies, disrupting normal functioning and creating a heightened sense of arousal. Unfortunately, some kids constantly live in this state. Like the twisted rubber band, when the pressure is released, it returns to normal. But, when it is stretched too far or for too long, the rubber begins to lose its elasticity, becoming brittle and cracked. Eventually, it breaks. That's similar to what happens to us when we experience excessive stress.

Consider what Dr. Archibald Hart said in his excellent book *Stress and Your Child:*

> Some stress is inevitable — even necessary — in everyday life. In order to function in the world, your child must stay alert, pay attention, and respond appropriately. He or she must go to school and learn. Certain tasks must be mastered and assignments must be completed. Play, too, involves certain challenges — learning to get along with other children, taking on new physical challenges, stretching mind and body. Every child must, therefore, embrace a certain degree of stress. But the stress problem begins when ordinary stress becomes too much stress.
>
> Think of the human body as a machine. Of course, a human being is more than this, but the analogy is fitting in that the human body, like a machine, was designed to carry out certain tasks in certain ways. And the human body, like every machine, has its certain built-in limitations.
>
> Take an electric motor, for example. If you examine the label on the motor of your washing machine or refrigerator you will notice that the phrase "duty cycle" is stamped on it, followed by a figure that is usually expressed as a percentage. The percentage refers to the amount of time the motor is designed to run. For example, a motor that is rated as "Duty Cycle 20 percent" is supposed to run only 20 percent of the time. If forced to run more

than this, it is likely to overheat and suffer increased wear and tear. If used continuously, the motor could burn out.

The human body and mind also have a "duty cycle." Our "motors" are designed for a certain amount of usage — stress, if you will. When the demand placed on the human machine exceeds this usage, the capacity for normal functioning will be exceeded; the result is "overheating" and increased wear and tear. And this overusage is what we commonly call stress. And this damage comes either from severely overloading the machine or from running a moderate overload for an extended period of time.[1]

What's stressful to one individual, however, may not be stressful to another. For some, stress means worrying about future events that cannot be avoided, and then worrying about them after they have occurred. For others, stress is simply the wear and tear of life. And still others see it as an overload of too many activities in their lives.

A certain amount of pressure and stimulation is necessary. Stress can be good if it is short-lived. Good stress is called *eustress;* it's derived from the Latin word *eu,* meaning good. It is positive and helpful because it has its limits and is not continuous. The body's equilibrium soon returns to normal. When the body does not return to normal rest and recovery, we have bad stress or *distress.*

WHAT CAUSES STRESS IN KIDS?

Stress in children can occur when something happens that:
- annoys them.

   List two annoyances that each of your children experiences.

   1.
   2.
- threatens them.

   List two threats that each of your children experiences.

   1.
   2.

- excites them.
  List two situations that excite each of your children.
  1.
  2.
- scares them.
  List two situations that scare each of your children.
  1.
  2.
- worries them.
  List two things that worry each of your children.
  1.
  2.
- hurries them.
  List two situations in which each of your children feels hurried.
  1.
  2.
- frustrates them.
  List two situations that frustrate each of your children.
  1.
  2.
- angers them.
  List two situations that anger each of your children.
  1.
  2.
- challenges them.
  List two situations that challenge each of your children.
  1.
  2.
- embarrasses them.
  List two situations that embarrass each of your children.
  1.
  2.
- reduces or threatens their self-esteem.
  List two situations that reduce or threaten the self-esteem of each of your children.
  1.
  2.

The normal changes and transitions of life can be enough

stress for just about anyone to handle. But when you add unanticipated changes, life can become even more difficult. A few examples of negative, unplanned, or unanticipated changes are parental separation or divorce, death within the family, injury or illness, a handicapped sibling or personal disability, alcoholism within the family, abuse, and multiple moves. But even more positive, normal changes can be a source of stress as well. Any change that affects your children needs to occur slowly with time allowed for kids to adjust.

In the 1960s, a major stress test was developed for adults by two physicians. This test is called The Holmes-Rahe Life Event Scale. It has been adapted for children and adolescents. Below, you will find 40 of the life events in that scale which apply to kids. They have been tailored to reflect situations in children's lives—for instance, the term *spouse* has been changed to *parent, work* to *school,* etc. The point value of each life event remains the same.

Life Events

1. Death of a parent	100
2. Divorce of parents	73
3. Separation of parents	65
4. Parents imprisoned	63
5. Death of close family member (grandfather, etc.)	63
6. Personal injury or illness	53
7. Parent's remarriage	50
8. Suspension or expulsion from school	47
9. Parents' reconciliation	45
10. Long vacation (Christmas, summer, etc.)	45
11. Parent or sibling illness	44
12. Mother's pregnancy	40
13. Sexual anxiety	39
14. Birth of baby (adoption)	39
15. New school, classroom, teacher	39
16. Family financial problems	38
17. Death or loss of close friend	37
18. Changes in studies	36
19. Quarreling with parents	36

20. Change in school responsibilities 29
21. Sibling going away to school 29
22. Family arguments with grandparents 29
23. Winning school or community award 28
24. Mother starting or stopping work 26
25. School beginning or ending 26
26. Family's living standard changes 25
27. Change in routines (bedtime, homework, etc.) 24
28. Trouble with parents (hostility, lack of communication, etc.) 23
29. Change of school schedule or courses 20
30. A family move 20
31. New school 20
32. New sport, hobby, or family activity 19
33. Change in church activities 19
34. Change in social activities (new friends, loss of old friends, peer pressure, etc.) 18
35. Change in sleeping habits (bedtime schedule, discontinuing naps, etc.) 16
36. Change in family get-togethers 15
37. Change in eating habits (starting or stopping a diet, new way of cooking) 15
38. Vacation 13
39. Christmas 12
40. A break in home, school, or community rules 11

When you total your children's points, it may surprise you how easily their scores can reach the 300-point level that indicates severe stress. Changes occur rapidly in kids' lives — far more rapidly than they occur for adults. For instance, six hours away from home each day in school can make kids vulnerable to experiencing life events numbered 8, 10, 15, 18, 22, 25, 27, and 31. The ups and downs of their social lives add the chance of stress from life events numbered 13, 17, 32, 36, and 39. Their high level of physical activity makes them especially susceptible to personal injury. They can easily contract a number of childhood diseases through their friends and schoolmates. And to make matters worse, some kids, because of their temperaments, become much more upset than others when encountering these life changes.[2]

Another main source of stress for our kids is competition. They encounter it everywhere—in the ads on TV, in organized sports, in their classrooms, and among peers. *Win at any cost* is the code by which they live, creating in them compulsions and a fear of failure. Their identities depend on their performances. This *drive* to be the best can dominate their lives at a time when learning to cooperate with others is far more important to their development.[3]

Some kids discover the rush of adrenaline-arousing activities at a young age, which can lead to stress as well as adrenaline addiction. We work with adults who are adrenaline addicts. They require a high level of activity and have a need to live on the edge of excitement and danger all of the time. High adrenaline in children can be caused by a number of conditions including too much noise, busyness, overcrowding, pressures, threats, television, and video games. None of us, though, were designed to live in this high state of arousal.

Many of the stresses in our children's lives can be avoided. It's best to deal with stress before it becomes distress. Most of the events that create stress can be categorized as either external or internal stressors. It helps if we can identify which category of stresses our kids are experiencing.

EXTERNAL STRESSES

External stress often involves conflict that may be expressed through open warfare (yelling and hitting) or a cold war (silent hostility and indifference).

1. Noise

Aggravating or loud noises create a stressful response even though kids may not be aware of them. One of the worst offenders is the high volume music our kids listen to constantly. Though they try to ignore the noise or seem unaffected by it, it takes its toll on them all the same. Try it for yourself. Sit in a noisy room and listen to all the sounds around you. How do they make you feel?

2. Television and video games

Television is a major source of stress. The rapid pace of frequently changing scenes, commercials, programs, and violence can be stimulating and stressful. Kids who watch TV or play video games hour after hour can become addicted to the flashing lights, sound effects, and violent themes to which they are exposed.

3. Overcrowding

Overcrowding is particularly problematic in urban areas. Rutgers University has conducted research on the effects of overcrowding on school-age children and adolescents. They monitored children who were put together in high density situations and discovered that crowding has negative physiological, behavioral, and sociological consequences. These kids became more competitive, tense, annoyed, and uncomfortable. And the effects were more obvious with boys than with girls.[4]

4. Environment

The effects of overcrowding stress is never more evident than in the gang warfare we're seeing more and more of in our cities. Each week several people are killed in Los Angeles because of gang activities. Often one or more of these victims are small children caught in the crossfire of rivaling gangs. In Southern California, one in nine parents won't allow their kids to play outside for fear they could be shot. In recent years in the Los Angeles area, we experienced the devastating disruption and trauma of rioting. This environment creates tremendous stress for our children.[5]

But environmental stress isn't something we only encounter when we step outside our front doors. We often create an environment within our homes that induces stress. Take the self-evaluation test below and find out the stress level in your home.

- Are you very strict; do you demand absolute obedience?
- Do you or others in your family shout a lot or overreact to situations?

- Do you or others tend to get angry a lot, or do you pout or blame others for your problems?
- Are you not a person of your word? Do you break your promises? Are you unreliable?
- Do you, as parents, reject those who are different and not allow them to be themselves?
- Are your children unable to get their dependency needs met with the family because there is not an atmosphere of love and unconditional acceptance?
- Do you or your spouse look to your children for your completion or, do you try to live out your dreams through your children?
- Is there someone in your family or in your extended family (aunt, uncle, or cousin) who humiliates, manipulates, intimidates, or exploits your children?
- Does your family have the no talk rule—you cannot talk openly about feelings, thoughts, or experiences that focus on pain or other negatives.

There are many more signs of family stress patterns, but if your family has any of these you need to do something about it. Begin by talking with your spouse about your concerns and then plan a strategy for change along the lines outlined in this book. If the tone of your home is really stressful—or if you have difficulty determining whether or not it is—then consider getting professional help.[6]

INTERNAL STRESS

There are a number of easily identifiable internal stressors.

1. Temperaments

One source of internal stress comes from parents failing to discover their children's unique personalities. It's impossible to interact with introvert children the same way you would interact with extrovert children. One of the most valuable things parents can do to reduce the stress in their kids' lives is to identify their individual temperaments and tailor their responses to their children accordingly.

2. Unrealistic expectations

Another common source of internal stress is unrealistic expectations. At an early age, kids develop expectations of themselves from their parents. Some are reasonable while others are not—for example, those created by parents who live out their unfulfilled dreams in their children. In some cases, kids simply have misconceptions about what their parents expect. Stress is created when the expectations don't match the children's abilities, interests, or sense of calling. The solution is to discover what your children think you expect of them and then clearly communicate reasonable expectations that are in harmony with who they are.

3. Sexual messages

Because of the contradictory messages our kids are bombarded with, sexual issues are a major cause of stress. Some messages say *it's better to wait* while others scream *do it now*. Some parents give their kids the message that sex is dirty while, at the same time, TV communicates that it's the greatest. It's important that we create a balanced, healthy attitude toward sexuality in our homes. By teaching positive sexual attitudes that are based on biblical values, we can prepare our kids to handle the mixed messages they hear from a non-Christian society.

4. Learned helplessness

Learned helplessness causes stressful problems for both boys and girls, but I've seen it happen more frequently in a father's relationship with his daughter. Fathers tend to complete tasks for their little girls without even being asked for assistance. It soon conveys the message to the daughter that she must rely on men to rescue her, so she learns to be dependent, helpless, and often manipulative as well.

All kids are dependent on their parents, but when that dependence is extreme or lasts too long, they may lose their motivation to become independent. Parents can counteract this pattern of learned helplessness by teaching their kids how to make wise decisions and giving them opportunities to make choices.[7]

STRESS FACTORS

Do you remember when you were in grade school? The fears, frustrations, uncertainties, and pressures? The following, listed according to age or grade level, are some of the most common things that cause kids at various stages of development to experience stress.

Birth to Five Years

Even very young children, from the age of birth to two years old, can experience stress. At this age stress comes primarily from children's parents and their environment. Infants and toddlers primarily depend on their parents for emotional stability. When they're upset, the calming influence of a parent is vital to their well-being. When parental stability is missing, however, infants tend to experience emotional storms while older children may respond with temper tantrums. Infants and toddlers are extremely sensitive to the emotional state of their parents. They assimilate their parents' moods, adopting them as their own. The feelings of an emotionally distraught parent can actually resonate within young children, upsetting them too.

Because of their limited development, children under five years of age lack social supports that could buffer them from their parents' emotional ups and downs. They can't talk with friends, or a teacher, or a church worker about what bothers them. They also lack the cognitive abilities to sort through their stressful experiences and disengage themselves from their parents' emotional upsets. In a very real sense, these kids are at the mercy of their parents' reactions to stress.

Stress issues at this age include shyness and stranger anxiety, learning to be autonomous and responding to discipline, learning to share, adjustments to day care, acceptance of younger siblings, fear of the dark and large animals, and aggression from other children.

How can a parent recognize stress in their young children? Kids send us warning signals in several ways. The main thing to watch for is a significant regression in your children's normal functioning. For instance, they no longer sleep well, they may stop crawling or walking, or they frequently whine, fuss, and cry.

The following list represents the warning signals of an infant or toddler responding to stress.[8]

Domain	Examples
Sleeping	Reverting to earlier patterns of sleep (usually more frequent nighttime waking); refusing to go to sleep, struggling to delay going to sleep; having nightmares.
Eating	Refusing foods that have been enjoyed; restricting intake to a few types of foods; returning to using a bottle after having been weaned; returning to liquids after having eaten solids.
Motor Activity	Giving up the large motor achievements of crawling, standing, walking, or running in favor of earlier patterns; giving up small motor achievements such as feeding himself, picking up and examining blocks, building block towers, and beginning to draw in favor of earlier ones.
Language	Reverting to crying or pointing instead of trying to name an object; giving up clear words for earlier versions such as going back to using ba for ball; giving up short sentences for single words; sounding babyish in tone of voice as she used to.
Toilet Training	Reverting to wetting or soiling instead of using the toilet; withholding stool; using places other than the bathroom, such as the living room, to relieve himself.

Emotional   Reverting to crying or clinging when a parent
Independence   leaves the room to go to another part of the
               house or leaves the child with a caregiver;
               becoming anxious and reticent with a care-
               giver instead of comfortably at ease; staying
               inside the house instead of playing in the
               yard or at a friend's house.

Kids at this age express their stress through anger, fear, or by becoming withdrawn or listless.[9] Another way young children indicate their stress is by overreacting to their experiences. For example, a three-month-old may cry more intensely when hungry. Or a six-month-old who normally enjoys bathing now cries. Or a 16-month-old who is building with blocks and enjoying herself suddenly knocks them down in anger.

The Grade School Years

In *kindergarten,* the main stressors are uncertainty, fear of abandonment by an important adult, fear of wetting themselves, and fear of punishment or reprimand from their teacher.

First grade stressors are fear of riding the bus and wetting themselves in class, teacher disapproval, ridicule from peers, receiving their first report card, and fear of not passing to the second grade.

In *second grade,* the stressors include not understanding a certain lesson, fear of the teacher's discipline, fear of being different in some way from other children in the class, and often, missing a particular parent.

Additional concerns for the five- to seven-year-old are learning to adjust to sitting still, learning to be competent in school skills, increased self-consciousness, fighting, and learning to handle rejections or failure.

In *third grade* stress is felt from fear of being chosen last on any team or for any activity, having to stay after school, a parent-teacher conference, fear of peer disapproval, fear of not being liked by the teacher, fear of taking tests, and not having enough time to finish a test or assignment.

In *fourth grade* the stressors are fear of being chosen last for anything, fear of peer disapproval of dress or appearance, fear that their friends will find new friends and share their secrets, fear of peer ridicule, and fear of not being liked by the teacher.

In *fifth grade* the stressors are just about the same as in fourth grade, but there is another concern as well — the possibility of not being promoted and thus not being a *big sixth-grader* the next year. In addition, the problem of increased competition, popularity, exposure to drugs and other substances, and confusion surrounding sexual development and sex roles.

In *sixth grade* there are some lingering and some new stressors, such as the fear of being chosen last for anything, peer disapproval of appearance, feeling unpopular, fear of the unknown concerning developing sexuality, and fear of not passing to junior high school (also the fear of going to junior high school).

These are just the stressors of school. When you add to this list all the things connected to the other parts of children's lives, you discover a multitude of possible stressors, and you realize that the potential for stress is all around them.[10]

WHERE DOES STRESS COME FROM?

Whether we are children, teens, or adults, most stress begins in our own minds. The most damaging stress comes from threats that cannot be acted upon since they exist only in our imaginations. Some children (and some adults too) imagine the worst in a situation. Their worrying creates even more of a threat and exaggerates their imagined fears. As parents, it's important to teach our kids to live by John 14:27: "Let not your heart be troubled, neither let it be afraid." Kids and parents who practice this Scripture will better handle the pressures of life — both real and imagined. But whether real or imagined, stress is a major contributor to worry and anxiety in our kids.

Do you understand worry? The word worry comes from an Anglo-Saxon root word meaning *to strangle* or *to choke*. Worry is the uneasy, suffocating feeling we experience during times of fear, trouble, or problems. It's the unnecessary fretting and stewing that keeps our minds stirred up and our stomachs churning. When we worry, we look pessimistically at the future, expecting the worst possible outcome to the situations in our lives.

Anxiety is the pervasive feeling of uneasiness, restlessness; it's a sense of dread or feeling that something is going to happen. But not all anxiety is bad; it can have a positive side.

A little anxiety in normal amounts can actually enhance performance. Athletes would be unable to perform successfully without it. It can strengthen concentration and spurs on the imagination, and produces more creative ideas.

But the negative aspects of worry and anxiety must also be differentiated from positive concern in troublesome situations.

Worry is like racing an automobile engine while it is in neutral. The gas and noise and smog do not get us anywhere. But legitimate concern . . . is putting the car into low gear on your way to moving ahead. You tell yourself that you are going to use the power God has given you to do something about the situation which could cause you to fret.

Worry immobilizes you and does not lead to action. But concern moves you to overcome the problem.

The Bible has a lot to say about this topic. Some Scripture verses describe the effects of fear, worry, and anxiety. And many other verses reveal that a worry-free life has many benefits. Notice the contrast in the verses below:

> I heard, and my (whole inner self) trembled, my lips quivered at the sound. Rottenness enters into my bones and under me—down to my feet—I tremble (Hab. 3:16, AMP).
> Anxiety in a man's heart weighs it down (Prov. 12:25, AMP).
> A tranquil mind gives life to the flesh (Prov. 14:30, RSV).
> All the days of the desponding afflicted are made evil (by anxious thoughts and forebodings), but he who has a glad heart has a continual feast (regardless of circumstances) (Prov. 15:15, AMP).
> A happy heart is a good medicine and a cheerful mind works healing, but a broken spirit dries the bones (Prov. 17:22, AMP).
> A glad heart makes a cheerful countenance, but by sorrow of heart the spirit is broken (Prov. 15:13, AMP).

Where do these feelings of anxiety and worry come from? Anxiety levels vary at different developmental stages throughout childhood. An infant notices the difference between his or her parents and another person and may become distressed when care-giving is transferred from the parent to someone else. Separation anxiety is one of the earliest and most common forms of anxiety in a young child, and if not handled correctly, can lead to fears of abandonment later in life.

A child experiencing anxiety can demonstrate a multitude of symptoms. These can include a racing or skipping heart, dizzy spells, lightheadedness, difficulty breathing, hyperventilation, being sick (nausea and chills), a feeling of tension, a choking sensation, tingling in parts of the body, and others.

Let's consider a day in the life of a child struggling with anxiety.

At ten years of age, Denise is quite bright and energetic, but she is handicapped by severe anxiety. Typically, Denise wakes very early. Her mind is racing, worrying about what the day will bring. Is her homework all done? What will happen in class? How will her friends treat her? Will her dress be just right? She hates playing jump rope; will her friends push her to play it again? These questions bug Denise even before she wakes up — or at least she feels that way. They never leave her at peace to get a full night's rest.

Breakfast is a chore for Denise because she usually doesn't feel like eating. If she eats too much, she gets nauseous and sometimes even throws up. If she doesn't eat enough, she gets weak and feels faint later. But who can eat when her stomach is all tied up in knots? And what if the bus is late? What if it doesn't come? What if today is really a holiday and she goes to school and no one is there? (Sometimes, Denise's mother tells her, her worries can be quite ridiculous.)

School itself is not too bad. Denise is good at school and usually gets through her classes quite easily. But recess is usually a pain because she starts worrying again. Will she fall and break an arm if she runs too much? What are her friends thinking? Why is that boy teasing her?

Denise's heart races. She feels a tightness in her chest. And sometimes she is overcome by thoughts of terrible things that might happen. Once, while playing, she was overcome by an intense fear that something had happened to her mother. She could not resist the urge and ran all the way home from school (several miles) to be with her mother. Then she felt so embarrassed she wanted to die.

And so Denise's day progresses. Right through to bedtime, it is filled with sometimes vague, sometimes specific, but always present worry. Obviously, the worry causes her a lot of stress. Headaches are frequent. Her stomach is almost in continuous turmoil. She is sick a lot. Unless she gets help, continuous anxiety is likely to torture her through adolescence and into adulthood.

Worry and anxiety is caused by a life filled with stress or trauma, being overprotected, rejected, living with anxious or worrisome parents, or too much pressure.[11]

We've mentioned numerous stressful situations, but let's consider some specific possibilities from a child's point of view. Listed here are twenty situations that produce stress in a child. Which do you think are the most stressful? Pretend you are a child and rank these in order from 1–20, with 1 being the most stressful and 20 being the least.

Children and Stress

____ Wetting pants in class
____ Having an operation
____ Giving a report in class
____ Having a scary dream
____ Being sent to the principal's office
____ Going blind
____ Moving to a new school
____ Going to the dentist
____ Being made fun of in class
____ Acquiring a baby sibling
____ Being suspected of lying
____ Being held back a year in school
____ Not getting 100 on a test
____ Getting lost
____ Receiving a bad report card

_____ Losing a game
_____ Hearing parents quarrel
_____ Being caught stealing
_____ Losing a parent
_____ Being picked last for a team[12]

How can you tell if your child is experiencing stress in his or her life? Sometimes we confuse misbehavior with the symptoms of stress and discipline rather than help our child.

Keep these symptoms in mind as you observe your child cope with anxiety.

- chronic irritability
- difficulty concentrating
- difficulty sleeping or staying awake
- poor eating habits, such as impulsive, uncontrolled eating
- restlessness
- rapid heart rate
- backaches
- neckaches
- headaches
- muscles aching for no apparent reason
- irritating behavior
- lack of spontaneity
- frequent mood shifts
- nervous habits, such as twitches, nail biting, pulling at hair, biting lips

If you notice these signs, especially a combination of them, you can be fairly sure your child needs help to learn to respond to life in a healthier manner.

Take a moment to consider the stress level of your child by using the following stress test.

Stress Test: Is My Child Overstressed?

Child's Name _____

Carefully review your child's behavior and complaints for the past two or three weeks and rate the following questions using this scale:

0 = My child infrequently feels or experiences this.

1 = My child sometimes (perhaps once a month) experiences this.

2 = My child experiences this often (between once a month and once a week).

3 = My child experiences this frequently (more than once a week).

_____ 1. My child complains of headaches, backaches, or general muscle pains or stiffness.

_____ 2. My child reports stomach pains, digestive problems, cramps, or diarrhea.

_____ 3. My child has cold hands or feet, sweaty palms, or increased perspiration.

_____ 4. My child has a shaky voice, trembles and shakes, displays nervous tics, or grinds and clenches his or her teeth.

_____ 5. My child gets sores in the mouth, skin rashes, or low-grade infections like the flu.

_____ 6. My child reports irregular heartbeats, skipped beats, thumping in the chest, or a racing heart.

_____ 7. My child is restless, unstable, and feels "blue" or low.

_____ 8. My child is angry and defiant and wants to break things.

_____ 9. My child has crying spells, and I have difficulty stopping them.

_____ 10. My child overeats, especially sweet things.

_____ 11. My child seems to have difficulty in concentrating on homework assignments.

_____ 12. My child reacts very intensely (with angry shouting) whenever he or she is frustrated.

_____ 13. My child complains of a lot of pain in many places of the body.

_____ 14. My child seems anxious, fidgety, and restless, and he or she tends to worry a lot.

_____ 15. My child has little energy and has difficulty getting started on a project.

_____ Total Score

How to rate your child's score.

0-5 Your child is remarkably low in stress or handles stressful situations extremely well.

6-12 Your child is showing minor signs of stress. While it is nothing to be concerned about, some attention to stress control may be warranted.

13-20 Your child is beginning to show signs of moderate stress. Some attention should be given to how your child copes with stress.

21-30 Your child is showing significant signs of stress. You should give urgent attention to helping him or her reduce stress levels.

Over 30 Your child appears to be experiencing very high stress levels. You should do everything possible to eliminate stressful situations until your child can learn to cope. You may want to consider getting professional help.

Note: You may want to go over the test items that have been answered with a rating of two or above to better understand the signs of stress in your child's life. See where you can provide relief and help your child build more resistance to stress. If you feel that your child's problems, no matter what his or her score on this test, are beyond your ability to handle, then seek immediate professional help.

IDENTIFYING SOURCES OF STRESS IN YOUR CHILD

Whenever you observe the symptoms of stress in your child, you need to identify the source. Look for its beginnings. You may want to ask yourself some of the following questions:

- What is the source of this stress? Is it within the family (such as Dad taking a new job that requires his frequent absence)? Or is it outside the family (perhaps failing a major math test)?

- Does the stress affect all the family members (as with a death), or just the child (having a close friend move away)?
- Was this stressful experience sudden (an accident or illness), or did it come on gradually (observing a close friend get sick and then die, or watching an older sibling become addicted)?
- What is the degree of the stress? Is it intense (a death of someone close) or mild (a cold which causes the child to miss a ball game)?
- Does this stressor require a short-term adjustment (arguing with a friend) or is it long-term (mononucleosis)?
- Was the situation expected (knowing a close friend is moving) or was it unexpected and unpredictable (a fire in the home)?
- Do the family members feel the stressor is one which can be adjusted to fairly soon (going to a new school) or is it beyond anyone's control (terminally ill parent with no prospects in sight for improvement)?

You will be able to help your child on a more long-term basis as you continue to be aware of every stressful situation. Each one carries with it both pain and potential for growth.[13]

Do you recall the "Children and Stress" test a few pages back? Following is how kids ranked these stress-producing situations. They are listed in the order in which the children perceived them, from most stressful to least stressful.[14]

KIDS RESPONSES TO "CHILDREN AND STRESS"

1. Losing a parent
2. Going blind
3. Being held back a year in school
4. Wetting pants in school
5. Hearing parents quarrel
6. Being caught stealing
7. Being suspected of lying
8. Receiving a bad report card

9. Being sent to the principal's office
10. Having an operation
11. Getting lost
12. Being made fun of in class
13. Moving to a new school
14. Having a scary dream
15. Not getting 100 on a test
16. Being picked last for a team
17. Losing in a game
18. Going to the dentist
19. Giving a report in class
20. Acquiring a baby sibling

Compare your answers with those of the children here. How close did you come? If you are like most parents, you will be surprised by the results. Does this make you want to listen more closely to your children?

Why not ask your own children to rank these in the same way for themselves? You may be surprised.

The symptoms of stress may not be as obvious with certain kids. In fact, your children may be having difficulty with stress without demonstrating the typical warning signs. The "Capable Kid Test" below was originally designed for children, but we believe it can be applied to teenagers as well. Use it as another means of identifying your children's attitudes and expressions of stress to help you monitor how they are doing.

The Capable Kid Test

Step 1 Think of a situation that your child or teen has experienced as stressful. It could be sharing a room or the car with a sibling, having a favorite weekend or a date canceled, flunking a test, not making the school team or play, being shunned by friends, or being embarrassed.

Step 2 Think about how your child reacted and whether that was his or her typical response to that type of situation.

Step 3 Choose one statement from the following list that best describes your child's reaction. (Select the first one that strikes you as appropriate.)

1. "Things like this always happen to me."
2. He or she becomes unusually quiet and walks away.
3. "I never get what I want. Nobody cares about me." (May become belligerent and verbally abusive.)
4. "Boy, am I disappointed." Then a few seconds later, "Oh, well, maybe it will work out the next time."
5. "This is no surprise. I was expecting something cruddy like this to happen." (Then becomes withdrawn and preoccupied.)
6. "That sure makes me angry, but I didn't know. Is there anything I can do about it now?"
7. "That is not fair. It's just not fair!" (And proceeds to have a child's or adolescent's temper tantrum.)
8. Doesn't visibly react, but just withdraws. Won't talk about it and tends to isolate himself or herself.

Step 4 Now, find the description of your child or teen as indicated below. (Remember, the description you select should be your child's typical way of responding.) This will clarify for you the level of ability your child or teen has to handle stress.

#4 or #6 — Either of these responses indicates a capable person. These kids handle stress well, will express disappointment or anger and then quickly figure out what to do about it. They will feel disappointed rather than greatly upset, and that disappointment will only last a few minutes.

#1, #2, or #7 — These kids are slightly vulnerable. They have upset reactions, but they don't last long. They soon calm down, become less preoccupied with themselves, and begin to find ways of handling the problem. They need to learn some new ways of coping to become less reactive.

#3, #5, or #8 — These kids are especially vulnerable. Their responses usually last more than 24 hours, and symptoms of being vulnerable are evident in their lives.

Here are some of the most important characteristics of capable children (or teens) and the vulnerable ones:

The Capable Child

- Resourceful
- Confident
- Able to confront people or situations when concerned or upset about something
- Willing to take risks
- Relaxed
- Responsible
- Able to express feelings easily
- Endowed with a sense of direction

The Vulnerable Child

- Withdrawn, preoccupied
- Often sick without an organic cause
- Isolated
- Secretive, noncommunicative
- Belligerent, uncooperative
- Overly sensitive
- In need of excessive reassurance[15]

10

Helping Your Children Handle Stress

One of the ways that you can help your children toward healthy emotional maturity is to teach them to identify stress in themselves. Childhood makes up a large portion of their lives, and during this time, they face some of the same stresses as adults—but they don't possess the same resources for dealing with them. You can help your children monitor their own lives by explaining to them what stress is and how to recognize the symptoms when it occurs.

If one of your kids came to you and asked, "What is stress?" or "How do I know when I have it?" what would you say? How would you describe stress to your child?

You could accurately answer, "Stress can result from what happens between people. Your friend may be mad at you, or the students in class may have made fun of you and it really hurt. It can also occur when you don't get enough sleep or when there is too much going on. In addition, you can create your own stress by what you think about yourself. If you think you're dumb or no good or not pretty, those ideas can cause stress."

When explaining what stress is to your children, you may want to use this "Have you ever. . . ?" approach:

Have you ever had your heart beat faster than usual?

Have you ever had your hands get cold and sweaty?

Have you ever had your stomach get tight like a knot?

Have you ever had your tummy hurt?

Have you ever felt nervous?

Have you ever felt sad or giggled a lot?

Have you ever felt mean, or like you wanted to cry, or get back at someone?

Have you ever had frightening dreams?

Have you ever not been able to concentrate?

Have you ever been grouchy?

Have you ever not gotten along with other people?

If children understand that these symptoms and others could be caused by stress, it will help them monitor themselves and use some of the stress reduction suggestions offered in this chapter.[1]

The best way to become aware of stress in your kids is by identifying the three main categories of stress.

TYPE "A" STRESS

The Type A category has two distinct characteristics—it is foreseeable and avoidable.

If a child plans to ride "The Cyclone" roller coaster or see one of the newest blood-and-gore horror films, he knows in advance the stress he will encounter and is able to avoid it if he chooses.

There are also foreseeable and avoidable stresses that are not under a child's control. Our world can be a scary place for kids. For instance, the world lives under the threat of running out of natural resources and seeing the environment become more and more polluted. And what about the ever-present possibility of nuclear war? During the Gulf War, many children were upset because one or both of their parents were called back to active duty in a war zone. And, parents whose jobs are threatened by our precarious economy pass this stress on to their children. These types of uncertainties are especially difficult for kids to handle.

TYPE "B" STRESS

Type B stresses come from demands that are neither foreseeable nor avoidable. These fall into the categories of crises, such as the death of a friend or family member or pet, an auto or sporting accident, the discovery of impending divorce or separation, or learning a sibling is gay or has AIDS. These stressful situations place the greatest demands on children because there is no way to gain control of them.

TYPE "C" STRESS

The third type of stressful situation, Type C, is foreseeable but not avoidable. A few examples of this kind of stress are: facing parents after being caught for truancy at school, taking an exam you didn't study for, taking a three-week trip with a family of five in a small car, and having a parent drafted into the military during wartime.

We as parents cannot eliminate all the stresses from our children's lives, but we can follow these guidelines in helping them cope with them.

1. Realize that your children live under constant stress.

2. Recognize stressors that the environment places on your child.

3. Take steps to eliminate stresses that are avoidable.

4. Teach your kids how to handle and deal with the stresses of life.[2]

How can kids cope with stress? They can follow the same principles recommended for adults dealing with stress.

1. Attempt to remove the source of the stress.

2. Refuse to allow neutral situations to become stressors.

3. Deal directly with the stressor.

4. Look for ways of relaxing that reduce tension.

Both adults and children can use these methods every day to combat stress. But let's look a little deeper into each of these areas and how they apply specifically to our children.

1. Attempt to remove the source of the stress.
Can children actually eliminate the stress? Too often they

don't have the necessary control to eliminate stressors on their own. In fact, kids often get stuck in a situation that becomes intense. They deal with it by inventing ways to avoid tension. For instance, kids may give up a friend because the friend's behavior is either contrary to their standards or it is frightening to them—or both. Or, during a family fight, kids might escape to their room and turn up the radio to drown out the noise. How does your child respond?

2. Refuse to allow neutral situations to become stressors.

As for neutral situations in children's lives, they sometimes get turned into stressors by other people. Exams in school are a case in point. Children's teachers and parents can be the source of acceptance or rejection for kids. Some children worry more than others about what people think of them. How do your children respond?

3. Deal directly with the stressor.

Is it possible for children to confront a stressor head-on and deal with it directly? To do this children will need to brainstorm some creative solutions to the situations that cause them stress. The child who is tired of being teased about being overweight may choose to diet and lose weight. Or a child who is constantly in trouble for talking in class may ask the teacher for a new seat assignment.

4. Look for ways of relaxing that reduce tension.

Learning to relax is one of the most important skills a child can learn when dealing with stress. But that's easier said than done. How do we teach our kids to relax when they're tense? Almost anything the child enjoys doing can be a relaxing activity.

Have you taken your kids to the public library and introduced them to the wealth of material found on the shelves? Learning to read and enjoy novels at an early age may provide one source of relaxation for them.

A common mistake that parents make is to schedule so many activities for their children that they have little time left just to be kids. After-school sports can often be overly competitive, putting an emphasis on winning instead of on fun and sportsmanship. Adults tend to be result-oriented and sometimes overlook the benefits of doing something purely for the joy of it—and they end up passing this attitude on to their kids.

Sometimes children are the best judges of what will help them handle stress. In a study conducted by the Ohio State University School of Nursing, 100 children were interviewed about how they coped with stress. More than 500 different methods for reducing stress were grouped into 13 categories and the children rated them for effectiveness.

The children unanimously agreed that the following responses were the least effective ways to deal with stress:

- Aggression which included yelling, screaming, swearing, tattling, talking back, and insults.
- Acting out emotionally which included crying, pouting, moping, punching, becoming angry, feeling sorry for themselves, and throwing a fit.
- Repetitive or habitual behavior which included cracking knuckles, twisting hair, biting nails, chewing gum, and compulsive eating.

The children chose the following three stress-relievers as the *most* effective:

- Social support which included talking to a parent, asking for hugs and help from parents, friends, and siblings.
- Cognitive behaviors which included thinking about a problem, talking to oneself, writing about it, working on a model, and planning what to do. Having positive thoughts was a very important item.
- Avoidance behaviors which included ignoring problems, changing the subject, and learning not to worry about the problem.[3]

How can we help our kids learn to handle today's stressors more successfully? One of the best analogies I've heard for helping a child is that it's like working on a jigsaw puzzle. You ask them to find the pieces; you point some of them out, and help them fit the pieces together.

SPEAK YOUR CHILD'S LANGUAGE

As parents, we need to learn to be flexible in our communication and speak our children's language. It's important to guide our conversations, especially with our young children, being careful to use clear statements, rephrasing for clarity. What may be clear to us simply may not register with our children.

Young kids have one-track minds, often focusing on one aspect of an event to the exclusion of all others. If you give them too much information at once, they can't handle it, so introduce new points gradually as they're ready for them. Your goal should be to help your kids organize their thoughts and explore all aspects and possible reasons for their stressful situations.[4]

When helping younger kids, remember these facts:

- Young children feel responsible for what has happened to initiate the stress;
- Young children make connections differently than adults;
- Young children are egocentric, seeing things only from a personal perspective;
- Young children have unrealistic and immature perceptions.

If this is how kids think, what can we as parents do to help them when they experience stress? First, I think we have to accept that at times it may not be possible to change their patterns of thinking. We may need to accept this fact to lessen our own frustration. The best thing we can do is help them fully express their inner thoughts and feelings because that helps them gain greater self-control in a crisis situation. By expressing their thoughts aloud, they can move to a new position and see the situation from a fresh perspective. By patiently repeating questions that encourage them to verbalize their thoughts, help them uncover the real or most probable reason for their stress. Try to help them discover this for themselves and watch for indications that they may be experiencing guilt.

IDENTIFYING YOUR CHILDREN'S NEEDS

Parents can help their kids handle the stresses of life by supporting them and teaching them coping skills. The following will help you with this goal by informing you of their needs:

1. Kids need caring, involved, and supportive parents. They handle stress much better if they know their parents are there for them.

2. A second resource is having a caring and loving extended family such as grandparents, uncles, aunts, etc. If these relatives are not available, a network of caring friends can take on a similar role.

3. Children need a safe and abuse-free environment, including protection from verbal and emotional abuse.

4. Children need supportive and understanding schools and teachers. Parents need to investigate the schools their children attend and become personally acquainted with the various teachers and their reputations. Even Christian schools need careful scrutiny—make certain they have a balanced approach and offer a healthy environment. Schools, churches, and homes can all be dysfunctional environments.

Dr. Archibald Hart has given a number of suggestions for helping kids who are experiencing stress in school.

- Don't put undue pressure on your child to make better grades than he or she is capable of making.

- Monitor the number of extracurricular activities with which your child is involved.

- Let your child talk about the anxiety. Sharing one's worries helps to relieve them.

- Watch for signs that a very young child is under stress at day care—unusually "clingy" behavior, regressing to an earlier stage of development, an increase in temper tantrums and other stress-related behavior.

- Arrange for tutoring or counseling if your child seems unduly stressed about grades or other school-related problems.

- Be alert to security problems at your child's school and be prepared to work with the school and other parents to solve these problems.

- Encourage your child to learn and practice a relaxation technique or a hand-warming exercise every time he or she is anxious about a school activity.[5]

5. Children need esteem-building activities. All kids need to develop a sense of competence and discover how important they are in the sight of God. Helping kids build an adequate identity is a theological issue, and solid and accurate teaching on this subject is essential. To do this, it will be necessary to limit the number of competitive and extracurricular activities in which the child participates.

6. Children need a supportive and caring church that ministers to the whole person and the whole family. Some parents are willing to drive a long distance for a church that ministers to a wide range of their family's needs and clearly presents the teachings of Christ. Be selective about where you worship so that your children develop a positive attitude and experience with their church. They can find in the church a source of strength and comfort during those difficult times in their lives.[6]

Children need time alone each week with their parents. This can be difficult to accomplish if there are several children in the family. At these times together, parents can practice their listening skills and help their children express their feelings and resolve their anger and frustration.

For years we've advised parents to inoculate their families in advance against stress to prepare them to handle sudden and unexpected events. Families who anticipate and plan for the major transitions they may experience, tend to handle changes more easily. While we can't insulate our kids from the problems and strains of life, we can help them build their resistance to stress. One of the best ways to do that is to gradually expose them to problems in a safe learning environment, so that when they encounter a real situation, they won't be devastated by it. As you do this, teach them skills to handle their problems.

While this means we have to avoid overprotecting our children, it doesn't mean overburdening them with situations they aren't ready to handle either. But we can be truthful with our kids about family difficulties and allow them to participate during a crisis. Over time, our children will develop the confidence, strength, and willingness to tackle the challenges they encounter.

Inoculating our kids means we won't be able to jump in to rescue them from problems as they grow older. Rushing out to replace a broken toy or lost pet does not promote their development. Teaching them to grieve is much more useful.

Teaching your children a healthy and positive pattern of self-talk is an excellent way to deal with life's stresses and build positive self-esteem as well. Parents can ask their kids questions that allow them to view their thoughts and to rephrase and reframe them to be healthier and more in balance.

I experienced burnout at one point in my life. It was nobody's fault but my own. I overcommitted myself, got too busy, and didn't allow enough time to recover. As parents we need to teach our children how to balance their lives and schedule recovery time. Let your kids know that after an intense experience, it's normal to feel a letdown. Parents may need to monitor their kids' schedules following a busy season or series of school or church activities to allow them free time for their bodies and emotions to recover.

One final suggestion is to teach your kids that they have the power to make choices and decide their priorities. Teach them to ask themselves whether a particular situation or activity is important enough to justify their investment of time, emotions, and energy. And tell them they have the power to choose their responses. Let them know that:

- if another person criticizes them, they have a choice whether they'll let it upset them or not.
- If someone wants them to do something or tries to pressure them, they have the choice whether or not they want to do it.
- If something doesn't go the way they want it to go, they can choose whether they'll be upset or not.[7]

There are some positive steps we can take to help our children overcome the problems that worry and create anxiety for them.

ANXIETY SEPARATION

Keep in mind that separation anxiety is most likely to occur (and is more intense) when a parent is gone for a long period of time. A brief separation is not usually a major problem if parents handle it wisely. Because of employment, day care, and kindergarten, short periods of separation between young children and their parents is unavoidable. A major consideration is the age of your children and the manner in which the separation occurs. The younger the children, the more careful a parent must be to make it a positive experience for them. After the age of five, most kids can handle some separation. And after three, the primary problem is anxiety, not just the physical separation.

Anxiety creates more anxiety. Sometimes the anxiety is as much the parents' as it is the children's. When this is the case, kids will tend to adopt their parents' stress as their own. To minimize the anxiety caused by your absence, here are some suggestions:

1. Take it slowly.

Take time to reassure your children before you leave and explain when you will return. It helps to develop rituals for separating, like *three kisses and a wave good-bye.* These rituals help to comfort your children and build confidence that you will return when you say you will.

2. Take time to familiarize your kids with their environment and care-giver.

If at all possible, spend some time with your kids in their new setting a few days in advance of the separation. They will be able to associate you with the new person and place.

3. Make your reunion a fun time.

Developing *hello* rituals—a long hug and a brief talk about the day or three winks—gives your kids something to look forward to. They need the comfort of a routine.

4. Don't sneak away.

Be up front and always say good-bye, even if your kids become upset. The best way to create anxiety is for them to suddenly realize you are gone.

5. Don't become angry if your kids protest your departure.

If your kids cling and fuss when you begin to leave, reassure them again that you will return. Give them an extra hug and a few extra moments before handing them over to the caregiver. If you begin to feel frustrated, remember that they probably will soon get over their distress.

6. Don't be irregular picking up your kids.

When kids have to wait for a parent, anxiety rises dramatically, so try to create some consistency in your schedule for picking them up.

7. Don't become upset if your kids try to punish you for being away.

If your children hide from you or demonstrate anger because you've been away, just accept their behavior as a sign of their love and allow some time to get reacquainted.[8]

You may find the following suggestions will help you guide your children through stressful times. They can be adapted and applied to various ages.

1. Look at the suggestions in the chapter on fear for tips that would apply to worry and anxiety.
2. Talk openly with your children about their worries and the physical sensations they experience when they are anxious.
3. Encourage your kids to keep track of their worries by making a list.
4. Work with your children to discover what is really causing their worry and anxiety. Help them troubleshoot, brainstorming several possible solutions.
5. Teach your kids simple, creative exercises for stopping stress. For instance, on one side of a 3" x 5" card they can write the word STOP in big letters. On the other side they write a Scripture verse, like Philippians 4:6-9. They carry the card with them, and when worry or anxiety strikes, they read the word STOP, then turn the card over and read the Scripture verse.

   Taking the card out interrupts their anxiety. Saying the word STOP further breaks the child's thought patterns and interrupts the impulse to worry. And reading God's promises becomes a positive substitute for worry.

6. Read the following Scripture passages to your children: Matthew 6:25-34; 1 Peter 5:7; and Isaiah 26:3. Ask your kids what they think these verses mean and how they would help them to not worry or feel anxious.
7. Monitor the activities that seem to contribute to your kids' stresses and anxiety. Sometimes a mere change in schedule and activity level can do wonders.

CHILDREN WHO COPE

Children who are able to cope with the stresses of life accept their strengths as well as their limitations. They are individualistic. While they have a number of friends and respond well to their peers, they are able to maintain their own individual identity. In contrast, peer-oriented children are less sure of themselves and have a lower opinion of themselves. Because peer pressure becomes so influential during adolescent years, preadolescent children must become aware of and be able to maintain their own identity.

Kids who cope are able to express their feelings. They can share their hopes, anger, hurts, frustrations, and joys. They don't bottle up their feelings.[9]

If your children struggle with these things, sit down with them and listen while they attempt to share their feelings of disappointment. Work with them, helping them discover some alternatives — anything from the ridiculous to the serious.

Eight-year-old Billy had planned to participate in his scout troop camping weekend. He came down with chicken pox two days before the trip and wasn't able to attend. He was terribly disappointed and upset. His mother told him, "Billy, I know you feel very bad right now, but I can think of five different ways you can handle this disappointment. One of them just might help. If you want to hear them, let me know."

In about 10 minutes Billy called his mother from his bed inquiring about her suggestions.

"You really want to know?" his mother asked.

Billy grumbled, "Yeah."

"Well," she said, "here they are. Maybe some are all right

and maybe some aren't." She shared with him the following:

1. You could throw your clothes out the window to show everyone how upset you are.
2. You could write a letter to God telling Him how disappointed you are and then read it to a friend.
3. You could call a few friends and complain to each of them.
4. You could set the timer on the clock and cry for forty minutes until the bell rings.
5. You could tell me how disappointed you feel and then we could talk about what we can do about it and maybe plan for this activity another time.

As a result of the mother's ingenuity, she had a very productive discussion with her son.

Like some adults, certain children are not as affected as others by the stresses of life. It may surprise you to discover that kids who are better able to handle their stresses have certain characteristics in common:

- They have an ability to concentrate rather than jump from one thing to the next.
- They can handle frustration.
- They are able to stick with a job until it is finished.
- They have learned to accept the disappointments of life, or they find alternatives.
- They are able to postpone gratification. This is an important skill for every child. Kids who handle stress well are those who are able to wait.

APPLYING THE WORD OF GOD

Helping your children understand, commit to memory, and apply passages from the Word of God is probably the most effective way to win the battle against stress.

A few of the passages which can become a source of stability and comfort to a child are:

> Consider it all joy, my brethren, when you encounter various trials, knowing that the testing of your faith produces endurance (James 1:2-3).

Be anxious for nothing, but in everything by prayer and supplication with thanksgiving let your requests be made known to God. And the peace of God, which surpasses all comprehension, shall guard your hearts and your minds in Christ Jesus. Finally, brethren, whatever is true, whatever is honorable, whatever is right, whatever is pure, whatever is lovely, whatever is of good repute, if there is any excellence and if anything worthy of praise, let your mind dwell on these things. The things you have learned and received and heard and seen in me, practice these things; and the God of peace shall be with you" (Philippians 4:6-9).

Fret not yourself because of evildoers. Be not envious toward wrongdoers. For they will wither quickly like the grass, and fade like the green herb. Trust in the Lord, and do good; Dwell in the land and cultivate faithfulness. Delight yourself in the Lord; And He will give you the desires of your heart, Commit your way to the Lord. Trust also in Him, and He will do it. And He will bring forth your righteousness as the light, And your judgment as the noonday. Rest in the Lord and wait patiently for Him; Fret not yourself because of him who prospers in his way, Cease from anger, and forsake wrath; Fret not yourself, it leads only to evildoing. For evildoers will be cut off, But those who wait for the Lord, they will inherit the land (Psalm 37:1-9).

The potential for stress is around all of us—but so are the solutions. The sooner our children learn to confront and handle the stresses in their lives, the better their quality of life will be.

Your Child's Self-esteem

We all have an opinion of ourselves, whether we think about it or not. Our self-image is the mental picture of our self-identity. It is the "I am" of each person. We either feel good about ourselves, or we dislike, or even hate and despise ourselves.

Where does our self-image come from? How does it develop? It is built upon clusters of memories. Very early in life we begin to form concepts and attitudes about ourselves, other people, and the world. Our self-concept is actually a cluster of attitudes about ourselves— some favorable and some unfavorable. Our minds never forget an experience. We may not be conscious of it, but it is still there.

To use a simple illustration, your children enter life carrying two containers—one in their left hand and one in their right. There is a plus sign on one container, and it collects all the positive information your kids receive about themselves. There is a minus sign on the other container, which holds all the negative information (these include sarcastic remarks, put-downs, looks of rejection, snubs, cruel statements, etc.).

If they gather more positives than negatives, they travel through life able to be productive and to experience joy and satisfaction. But if they collect more in the negative container than in the positive, they move through life off-balance. Their self-image and sense of self-worth can become distorted, and they struggle to gain their equilibrium.

Your kids have memories of situations in which they feel valuable and important and others that are not so pleasant. They may have experienced the pain of being rejected in front of a class at school or of you scolding them in front of their friends. Or maybe they spent hours building something only to have it not work or other people criticize it. They may have walked into a new school and no one talked to them for several days. Memories, both good and bad, form self-image.

Years ago we visited an old-fashioned carnival funhouse with a hall of mirrors. It was a hilarious experience. Some of the mirrors made us look fat and squat, others thin as a thermometer. The mirrors reflected countless distorted images everywhere we looked. Finally, at the end was a regular mirror that reflected our normal image.

Some people pass through life never perceiving their normal image. They live with constant self-distortions. These distortions filter messages and comments that would bring their own evaluation into proper perspective. Some of our mirrors distort us by reducing our value. Others distort us by overestimating our value.

The Scriptures reflect us as we really are. But too often we forget or neglect consulting this reflection. We need a constant reminder of who we really are. It is not our evaluation of ourselves that counts, nor that of our friends or parents, but God's evaluation which brings clarity to the mirror.

What is it that reflects your kids' self-image? What is the origin of their self-esteem? For most, an important influence is the relationship they have with their parents. A parent's love is the most important source of self-esteem. Kids who do not experience love and acceptance from their parents, have difficulty loving or accepting love from other people. Because they never felt the commitment of their parents, they also have trouble making commitments to others. They move through life searching for love and commitment. Their need is insatiable—they can never get enough love and commitment. Or they live in fear of losing the love they have while, at the same time, they behave in a way that pushes people away. Still others are not willing to risk rejection, so they never become involved in relationships that could provide the love and commitment they crave. This is why parents play such a significant role in their kids' images of themselves.

The words self-image and self-esteem are used frequently, but are just as frequently misunderstood. When we talk about self-esteem, we are not referring to egotism or a conceited or inflated perspective of self. *Webster's* describes self-esteem as "confidence and satisfaction in oneself." It is a sense of one's own value and worth. It has nothing to do with egotism, which *Webster's* describes as "the practice of speaking or writing of one's self in excess." In other words, egotism is a distorted sense of one's importance. This is reflected in Proverbs 16:18 which states, "Pride goes before destruction, a haughty spirit before a fall." The basis for the self-esteem that we are suggesting is rooted in the Word of God. Our identities, worth, and value come because God created us, and because we have true identity through Jesus Christ.

The foundation for our self-esteem is theological. We have been created by the hand of God and in His image. There may be days we don't feel like that's true, especially if it's been a particularly difficult day. But, nonetheless, it is a fact.

CREATED IN GOD'S IMAGE

We are created in God's likeness (see Genesis 1:26). How are we made like God?

God created Adam and Eve with an inherent goodness. They were not morally neutral. God was pleased with them, for Genesis 1:31 says, He "saw all that He had made, and behold, it was very good." But then Adam and Eve sinned. When sin entered the world, it marred our God-image but did not destroy it. And this God-image is the basis of our value, worth, and dignity. That's why we can respond to our children in ways that will help them develop a positive and healthy self-esteem. Your child is worthy. Regardless of his or her age, your child is a product of God's handiwork.

Take a look at your children some night while they are sleeping and read Psalm 139:13-18 out loud. What does this passsage tell you about the worth of both you and your children to God?

> For You created my inmost being; You knit me together in my mother's womb. I praise You because I am fearfully and wonderfully made; Your works are wonderful, I know that full well. My frame was not hidden from You when I was made in the secret place. When I was woven together in the depths of the earth, Your eyes saw my unformed body. All the days ordained for me were written in Your book before one of them came to be. How precious to me are Your thoughts, O God! How vast is the sum of them! Were I to count them, they would outnumber the grains of sand. When I awake, I am still with You.

God wants your children to grow up realizing that their worth and value have been decreed, not by this world, but by God Himself!

THE ROLE OF SELF-ESTEEM

Why is your children's self-esteem so important? Because it is going to affect just about every area of their lives.

How kids feel about themselves affects their attitude. Children with strong self-esteem have better attitudes about school, friends, home, parents, and church. The higher value kids place on themselves, the more they value the people and things in their lives.

Self-esteem affects your kids' health. If they feel good about their bodies and value them, they are less likely to abuse them with drugs and alcohol. It's extremely important that our kids learn to love and care for their bodies.

Kids with healthy self-esteem tend to be more honest. Kids with low self-esteem tend to step over the lines of propriety. They rationalize, *If I don't care about myself, why should I care what others think of me?* or *If I'm not important, why is it so important to follow these dumb rules?*

Self-esteem is tied into how well our kids get along with others. Years ago I heard the philosophy that *you cannot be happily married to another person unless you are happily married to yourself.* There's a lot of truth in that statement, because it is difficult to get along with others if you don't first get along with yourself.

Self-esteem affects schoolwork as well. School will be a problem when a child thinks, *Why bother? What difference does it make?* or *I'm dumb and I can't get any attention by working hard. I might as well make a disturbance. At least I can get some kind of attention that way.*

IDENTIFYING YOUR CHILD'S SELF-ESTEEM

The following lists give some characteristics of children with positive self-images and children with negative self-images. Evaluate the self-esteem of your children as you read these traits.

Children who have a positive self-image:
- are happy children.
- feel they are liked by peers.
- are able to make friends.
- are able to tell you some things that they are good at.
- feel strong and capable.
- feel secure in their home.
- feel like important people.
- are able to give of themselves to others.
- feel good that they are doing their best in school.
- do not measure their importance by grades and accomplishments.
- feel like important members of their families.
- accept their physical appearances and generally like how they look.
- attempt new tasks with courage.
- tend to be creative in their own special ways.
- show love and kindness to others.
- participate in games with other children rather than just watch.
- feel accepted for their uniqueness.

Children who have a negative self-image:
- may be unhappy much of the time.
- may cry, whine, or withdraw.
- may not feel liked by their peers.
- may find it difficult to make friends.
- may feel that they have to compete at home for attention.
- may feel that they are in trouble much of the time.
- may not know their own special abilities or talents.
- may have lots of conflicts with peers or adults.
- may not feel like important members of their families.
- may not attempt new tasks because they fear failure.
- may feel they are only important if they perform well.
- do not show love and kindness to others.
- may watch other children playing but won't participate.
- may be extremely competitive with other children.
- are often mean to other children.
- may feel that they are a disappointment to others.
- may be afraid to volunteer answers in a group situation.
- may be extremely shy.
- may worry a lot.[1]

Are children born with or without self-acceptance? I like what Bruce Narramore has to say:

> When a child is born, he has neither a physical, nor an emotional self-image. He is simply a bundle of possibilities waiting for his innate potential and the influence of his environment to mold him into an independent person. And he is about to begin a journey that will shape his entire attitude toward himself. The way he makes this journey, and the help he gets along the way, will determine the essential make-up of his self-concept.[2]

WHAT DETERMINES SELF-ESTEEM?

Children's first self concepts begin in infancy. Love, acceptance, and a positive environment all contribute to their sense of who they are. Toward the end of their first year, kids have started to fashion a mental image of who they are.

Part of the struggle we have as parents is that our own feelings about our kids tend to fluctuate. It is easier on some days to be positive, affirming, and loving than it is on other days. Our feelings help to develop our children's sense of worth, confidence, and value. But sometimes what we do and say tends to hinder this development. Sometimes nicknames or labels that parents give their children linger for years. Bruce Narramore describes some of the labels people in a seminar remembered their parents giving them as children. They included words like *tank, motor mouth, leather gut, beanpole, pea brain, simple Sally, fat cow's tail, elephant ears,* and *devil daughter.* These kinds of nicknames not only hurt—they are damaging. Consider this about labels and nicknames.

> Whenever a child is labeled, an image is written on his mind. Repeated labels influence a child who is shaping an image of himself. Accusations such as "clumsy" or "stupid" become important elements of the child's growing attitude toward himself. Absorbed and stored in his mind, these labels act as a barrier to his development of self-esteem.
>
> Frequently these labels become so deeply embedded in our personality that they continue to exist even when there is no basis for them. A girl who is teased about her looks, for example, may never learn to like her appearance even after she has become a beautiful woman. A man labeled "stupid" as a child may still feel foolish even though he has a string of college degrees and has proven himself in business. The curse of childhood labeling and ridicule was clearly expressed to me by an attractive woman who said, "I don't care how beautiful people think I am. To me, I'm still an ugly girl from the wrong side of the tracks." Childhood ridicule overruled the reassurances of her friends because a contradictory image had been etched in her mind.
>
> However, each time parents communicate respect, love, and trust to their child, they lay another building block in the foundation of that child's self-esteem. Praise, genuine acceptance, patience, and affirmation go a long way in helping a young child to cultivate a good attitude toward himself. Such responses from parents and other people help to form the roots of the child's self-acceptance.[3]

We hear so much about victimization today—citizens victimized by criminals, spouses victimizing each other in marriages, etc. Many of our children grow up feeling victimized, because of the discounting messages they receive from their parents. I constantly hear about parental victimization from adult children in my counseling, and unfortunately, this contributes to a child's low self-esteem.

One middle-aged woman told me, "I felt victimized most of my life. Oh, nothing dramatic happened to me when I was a child. I wasn't physically or sexually abused. But my mother was critical of me so much of the time. And whenever she said something nice, I couldn't believe it because the compliments were surrounded by so many discounting statements. Dad just wasn't available to me. He didn't want to talk or play with me. He was around physically, but I felt emotionally abandoned. I grew up wondering what was so wrong with me to keep him from being part of my life."

Children who grow up receiving discounting messages believe they deserve these messages. They learn to cope by blaming themselves for the criticism, abandonment, and discounting they receive. By the time they reach adolescence and adulthood, they may be relatively free from their parents' critical messages. But they have internalized blame to such an extent that they now discount themselves. They make statements of denial, criticism, and blame to themselves like: *I can't do anything right. What a dummy! I should have done that differently. There must be something wrong with me if the teacher has to show me the same formula over and over.* These statements reflect a self-image in trouble.

We parents sometimes unknowingly set the stage for this to occur in our children. We have no idea how powerfully our words, tone, and actions influence our children. Consider these insights from the Book of Proverbs.

There are those who speak rashly like the piercing of a sword, but the tongue of the wise brings healing (Proverbs 12:18, AMP).

Death and life are in the power of the tongue and they who indulge it shall eat the fruit of it (Proverbs 18:21, AMP).

Do you see a man who is hasty in his words? There is more hope of a (self-confident) fool than of him (Proverbs 29:20, AMP).

When we ignore our children—deny the severity or importance of their life events, the solvability of their problems, or their ability to succeed—they internalize their feelings and grow up limited and struggling with low self-esteem. When we criticize them, they grow up criticizing and abusing themselves.

Here are several common examples of discounting messages that lead to this problem. Can you identify the denial, criticism, abandonment, and abuse in these examples?

- Your child is selecting something at the store to buy with his allowance. You keep saying, "Are you sure that's what you want? Once you buy it, we're not bringing it back."
- You make fun of your child for being afraid of a large dog.
- You berate your child for losing a fish as he was trying to pull it into the boat.
- You tell your child, "You're going to turn out just like your rotten father."
- You ridicule your adolescent son for being bashful around girls.
- You make fun of your child's visible handicap or weakness in front of other children or your adult friends.
- You tell your six-year-old, "I will love you if you're a good boy."
- You say to your child, "If you get good grades and are quiet around the house, Daddy and I won't fight as much."
- You tell your 14-year-old boy, "I don't have time for you when you behave this way. Go to your room until you figure out what's wrong with you."[4]

Children who grow up on a steady diet of these kinds of messages will internalize an incredible knack for blaming themselves for situations which are not their responsibility. Instead of becoming mature, independent, self-confident individuals, their adult lives will be marked by self-blame, self-doubt, and insecurity.

HOW TO BUILD A HEALTHY SELF-IMAGE

If you are the conveyor of negative messages to your children, it's very likely that you were the recipient of negative messages from your parents as a child. To some degree, you adopted a discounting self-attitude. But the pattern can be broken.

The first step in breaking this cycle is to become aware of your own thought patterns. Do you ever deny the existence or severity of a problem in your life? Do you ever deny your ability to solve a personal problem? Are you overly self-critical? Do you blame yourself for situations which are not your responsibility? Do you abuse yourself verbally? How is your own self-esteem?

A negative tendency is often so ingrained that it is an automatic response. Bringing it to the surface will take some work on your part, but the results will be worth it. Realize that you are not doing this to increase your guilt or to be hard on yourself. You are simply trying to discover how much of your behavior is motivated by discounting yourself.

One way to determine if this is true for you is to track your responses to the problems you encounter. Ask yourself several times a day: *Am I ignoring a problem which really exists? Am I overreacting to the problem? Have I asked for help in solving the problem? Did I avoid the situation because I didn't think I could solve it?*

The good news about this negative thinking pattern is that it can change; you can break the cycle in your family. But first you must become an explorer of your own attitudes and responses. Once you identify your own thought patterns, you are free to choose alternative nurturing approaches or solutions. What you learn about yourself will help you change your discounting responses toward your children.[5]

Nurturing messages are those which convey to your children something good about themselves. These positive messages don't increase their value; they are already priceless in God's eyes. But nurturing messages increase your children's value in their own eyes, thus opening the door for learning, growth, maturity, independence, and a healthy self-perspective.

We need to nurture our children every day. Casual, spontaneous comments and planned, direct, eye-to-eye statements are equally effective. Nurturing involves giving more affirmation than corrections.

Your pattern for responding to your children can be best summed up in two passages from God's Word. The first is Colossians 3:21. "Fathers, do not provoke or irritate or fret your children—do not be hard on them or harass them; lest they become discouraged and sullen and morose and feel inferior and frustrated; do not break their spirit."

The *Amplified* version tells us so clearly the results of discouraging words. The other side is found in 1 Thessalonians 5:11. "Therefore encourage one another and edify— strengthen and build up—one another, just as you are doing."

Encouragement comes through praising. All children need to be praised for their efforts, for improving, and for just being who they are as individuals. Praise your kids when they least expect it. Even young children, who as yet have no vocabulary, will pick up your praise from your tone of voice and nonverbal communications. It's your attitude that speaks to them.

One mother said she hugged her infant when he was learning to stand, whether he stood for two, six, or ten seconds. A father said he made it a point to praise his daughter for every effort she made—even if it was only a 20 percent effort. In time, he noticed that she began to become more persistent and didn't give up as easily. It's important as a parent that you look for things to praise.

Years ago I worked with a mother who was having difficulty with her child. The mother was concerned because her daughter was demonstrating poor behavior and a low self-esteem. I tried an approach I had never suggested before. Each day the mother was to keep a record of each time she criticized her daughter. I was shocked the next week when she walked into my office and literally threw several sheets of paper at me. "It's not you I'm upset with," she moaned. "It's me. I couldn't believe how many times I criticized my daughter. No wonder she's responding the way she is. She's not the problem, I am!"

With many parents I've suggested that if you do criticize, do it in a way that will be accepted. How? It's actually quite simple. In place of focusing on the behavior that you don't like or want to eliminate, direct your attention (and theirs) to what it is you want them to do. There is a greater likelihood that your children will change when you focus more on what you want them to do rather than reinforce what they have been doing. If you make a point each day of sharing with your children messages that nurture, it will soon become automatic. It works!

Nurturing shows your kids that you believe in their capacity to learn, change, and grow. Nurturing shows that you are aware of the kind of picture you want your kids to have of themselves. Their minds are like computers. Every message you send to them goes into one of the two files: discounting or nurturing. And the file with the most data will determine how they see themselves. When nurturing occurs on a regular basis, it's difficult for low self-esteem to gain a foothold in your child's mind.

I like the story that Kevin Leman shares about his own experience when he was twelve. He was selected as the starting third baseman for his All-Star Little League game. In the third game the teams battled to a tie, and Kevin's team needed one more out to send the game into extra innings.

A ground ball was hit and the shortstop executed a perfect throw to Kevin at third base for a force-out. It was a good throw. There was no sun in his eyes. But another player bumped into him and he dropped the ball. It just popped out of his glove and the other team won the game. He felt totally deflated and tears began to fill his eyes.

Fortunately, he had a manager who was a wise man and knew how he must be feeling. He walked over to Kevin, put his arm around him and said, "Kevin, if it hadn't been for you we never would have made it this far, and I want you to remember that. You've been doing a good job all year, so keep your head up."[6]

Is this how you respond to your children when they mess up? Did you ever have anyone respond to you this way when you were a child and made a mistake? This is nurturing. This is encouragement. This is believing in another person.

Messages that nurture are based on unconditional love,

which parents must work at, especially if they grew up in a negative home instead of a nurturing family. But you can rely on Jesus Christ to fill the void in your life with His presence and help you learn how to love unconditionally as He loves you.

Let's look at two types of nurturing messages that will help develop healthy, self-disciplined children. The first category is affirmation and compliments, given for your children's good behavior and right choices. The second category is nurturing messages of correction for bad behavior and wrong choices.

It is easier for most parents to affirm positive behavior than to deal with negative behavior in a positive way. But we must continually remind ourselves to convey nurturing affirmations and compliments such as:

"You treat your friends very nicely."

"You have a wonderful ability with tools."

"Thanks for doing such a good job on your chores today."

"Your schoolwork has really improved."

"I like the way you cleaned your room. Thank you."

"You're a very special person to me."

"I'm so glad you're my child."

"I love you because you deserve to be loved. You don't have to earn it."

"You make my life more complete just by being you."

"I'm glad I have you. You teach me so much about life."

Such affirmations cause kids to realize, *Mom and Dad really love me. They think I'm a lovable person. My needs are important to them. They want to help me face my problems and solve them. What happens to me is very important to them. They trust me to think for myself and make good decisions.*

As you convey nurturing messages, be sure your value judgments are attached to your children's behavior instead of their person. For example, a toddler exploring the family room approaches the television, which is within his reach. Fascinated by the shiny knobs and switches, he reaches out to touch the TV. His mother says, "Don't touch, Joshua. Remember, I said you can look at the television, but you can't touch it. Here are some things you can touch." She jiggles a box of toys. Joshua stands in front of the TV for a moment wrestling with the temptation. Then he turns away toward the toys.

What would you have said to affirm Joshua? Many of us would remark, "Good boy, Joshua!" And if he had touched the TV against his mother's wishes, it would be, "Bad boy, Joshua!" But those kinds of statements are value judgments on Joshua. He soon learns that he is sometimes good and sometimes bad, which confuses his self-perception.

Instead, Joshua's mother said, "Good choice, Joshua!" She wants him to learn that he is capable of making good choices, for which he is affirmed, and bad choices, for which he is corrected. But Joshua is always regarded and nurtured as a good boy. This subtle, but important distinction can make a world of difference in your child's self-image.

When your children make wrong choices or misbehave, they need to be corrected. But since we are concerned with nurturing them at all times, corrective messages must be delivered in a positive, affirming way. We don't correct our children to make them feel bad, but to help them discover a better way to do something. Here are a few examples of nurturing statements of correction:

"Here is a way you can do it that you might like better."

"It sounds like it's hard for you to accept a compliment. Perhaps you need more practice accepting them, and I need more practice giving them."

"I'm not sure you heard what I said. Tell me what you heard, and then let me repeat what I said if you heard differently."

"Listen to the help and care I'm giving you right now."

"You can't do that any longer, but you can do this instead."

"That was a poor choice you made, but I have some good ideas you may want to consider for getting back on track."

"You're not paying attention. Something must be on your mind, since you are so good at listening and thinking. I wonder what it is."[7]

What steps can you follow to help your children develop a healthy self-esteem? The first is to teach them the Word of God at an early age, focusing on who they are in Christ. Children who grow up with a healthy and accurate understanding of God and how He views them will have a good basis for self-acceptance. Here is a sampling of such messages. How do they make you feel about yourself? How will your children feel about themselves if these thoughts and concepts are taught to them?

Scripture Reference	God's Message to You as a Believer
Genesis 1:26-27	I am uniquely created in God's image.
Matthew 5:13	I am the salt of the earth.
Matthew 5:14	I am the light of the world.
Luke 11:9-10	I ask and receive; I seek and find; I knock and the door is opened unto me.
John 8:32	The truth has set me free.
John 14:27	I have peace.
John 17:18	I have been sent into the world.
John 17:22	I have God's glory.
Acts 13:38	I have forgiveness of sins through Christ.
Romans 8:1	I now have no condemnation.
Romans 8:32	I have all things.
Romans 12:6	I have been given gifts.
1 Corinthians 2:16	I have the mind of Christ.
1 Corinthians 3:9	I am God's fellow worker; I am God's field, God's building.
2 Corinthians 4:16	My inner self is being renewed day by day.
Ephesians 3:20	I have a power source within me which is able to do exceeding abundantly beyond all that I ask or think.
Philippians 4:7	The peace of God guards my heart and mind.
Philippians 4:13	I can do all things through Him who strengthens me.
Philippians 4:19	God shall supply all my needs according to His riches in glory in Christ Jesus.
2 Timothy 1:7	For God has not given me a spirit of timidity, but of power and love and discipline.
Philemon 6	The knowledge of every good thing is in me.
1 Peter 2:9-10	I am chosen.

How do you direct children's thoughts so they begin thinking about themselves in a positive way? One way is through a series of questions which you weave into your everyday conversations with them. These questions are simple and yet in time could have an effect upon their perspective. You could ask:

"What was something you did today that you felt good about?"

"Tell me about something you really enjoyed today."[8]

Sometimes I run into parents who express concern over the fact that their children seem unable to handle praise or a compliment. They seem embarrassed and awkward when it's given and appear to discount the praise. For kids who are struggling with their self-esteem, this is not uncommon. Some children will disagree with the praise, shrug, ignore the statement, argue with you, or give someone else the credit for what happened.

Accepting criticism is easier for some children, because it reinforces what they believe about themselves. When you were a child did anyone give you guidelines for accepting a compliment or handling praise? Probably not. Most of us weren't given any help, or at the most, we were told to just say "thank you." Unfortunately, just saying "thank you" can become so automatic that we don't even hear ourselves saying the words.

Perhaps the best way to teach a child how to accept a compliment or praise is by modeling for them our own responses to compliments. As children learn to respond appropriately to a compliment (even though they feel uncomfortable and awkward), they will in time feel better about themselves because of these positive responses. Here are some guidelines you can teach your children and eventually these will become very natural for them.

- Don't ignore the complimenter.
- Don't downgrade the compliment.
- Don't question the motives of the complimenter.
- Don't mock the compliment.
- Don't question the intelligence of the complimenter.
- Don't question the sanity of the complimenter.
- Don't give the credit to someone else.

- Don't shrug.
- Don't look down at the floor.
- Don't turn around.
- Don't walk away.
- Don't look pained.
- Don't look confused.
- Don't say, "Who me?"
- Don't whisper.
- Don't mumble.
- Don't say, "You're kidding."
- Don't giggle.
- Don't run for cover.
- Don't say, "But it was an accident."
- Don't say, "But I could have done better."
- Don't say, "But it's no big deal."
- Don't say, "Yes, but. . . ."
- Don't say, "Maybe, but. . . ."
- Don't say, "OK, but. . . ."[9]

Use statements like "Thank you. I appreciate your telling me that." Or, "Thank you. I'm glad you noticed and told me." Or, "Thank you. It helps me to hear that."

When you first begin teaching your children to do this, accept their responses without corrections. They may mumble and even look away. Reinforce and praise all of their efforts. In time, they will be more definite in words and tone and even their nonverbal expressions. One mother said she made a game out of this approach with her preschooler. She said to her five-year-old, "Janice, I'm going to tell you something that I like about you, and let's see what you can say back to me. I think you'll like this game."

A father used this approach with his eight-year-old son, "Jim, I'm going to give you some compliments and show you a new way to accept them. As you learn this I think you are going to feel better about yourself."

I told Arthur's father how great it was that he was helping to improve Arthur's self-image. He said, "Thank you. It's nice of you to recognize how hard we've been trying."

I knew Arthur was in good hands.

Most of us have no idea how to accept a compliment correctly. We're afraid that if we agree with the person who complimented us, we'll sound conceited. Sometimes, just thinking about the compliment can make us feel self-conscious. So we look down at the floor. We turn around. We blush or give a *who, me?* look. We don't say thank you. Or if we do, we whisper or mumble it. We give credit to everyone but ourselves. And we question the complimenter's motives *(Why would he be saying that about me? He must want something.)* or sanity *(She's crazy if she thinks that.)*.

Criticism, which reinforces what we believe about ourselves, is easy for us to accept. In fact, it sometimes stays with us for days, weeks, and even years. But praise goes in one ear and out the other. We discount it, ignore it, and disown it.

Some of us feel starved for praise. Ironically, we may be getting all the praise we need. But we don't hear it. We dismiss it or shrug it off before it can have a positive effect on our self-image.

Praise can only make your children feel better about themselves if they learn to accept it. The rules for doing that are pretty simple — you can teach them to your kids in a couple of days. But first, you'll need to learn them yourself and begin using them in front of your kids. When it comes to accepting praise, what you *do* may affect your kids even more than what you *tell* them.

Learning to accept compliments will have a dramatic impact on your children's self-image. One day they will just be following the rules mechanically; the next day they'll be following them naturally, and feeling better about themselves.

Section
Three

Dealing with our own responses to our children's emotions.

Endnotes
Additional Reading Resources

12

Dealing with Your Emotional Responses to Your Children

"I can't believe I blew it again," Karen said in a discouraged and defeated voice. "I feel like a total failure. I have these good intentions and great expectations and then, once again, some little thing happens and I lose it."

Karen is a committed Christian woman who loves her husband and two children. One of the greatest desires of her heart is to be a great mom. She wants to give her kids a different kind of model than she had in childhood. But for several years Karen has struggled with a low frustration tolerance and a short fuse when dealing with her children.

"I've gone to seminars, listened to tapes, and read books about how to be an effective parent. Most of the time I do a great job. But when I lose it and start dumping on the kids, I feel like all the good I've accomplished has been undone. It's so discouraging."

Over the years, we've talked with hundreds of parents who have expressed feelings and concerns similar to Karen's. If you've read this far in the book, it's obvious that you understand and appreciate the importance of healthy emotional development. You are committed to raising emotionally healthy children. You love your kids and want God's very best for them. However, there is still one more area that needs to be addressed. And it's not about your children—it's about you.

It's one thing to help your children understand and deal with their emotions. But one of the most challenging aspects of parenting is learning how to deal with the emotions you have in response to your children's emotions. It's one thing to help your children develop healthy emotional patterns. It's a significantly greater challenge to deal with your own emotional responses to your kids.

Read through the following statements. Do any of them sound familiar to you?

"How many times have I told you not to interrupt when I'm on the phone?"

"Christopher, I'm sick and tired of your leaving a mess all over the house. This may be hard for you to believe, but I'm not your personal maid."

"If the kids don't stop fighting, I'm going to commit myself."

"You are in real trouble now. Just wait until your dad gets home."

"If I've told you once, I've told you a hundred times. Don't take things out of this drawer without asking."

"I've had enough. If this happens again, you're in serious trouble. I'm not kidding. I really mean it this time."

Have your ever heard parents make statements such as these? If we're honest with ourselves, we've all probably made statements similar to these. If you've been a parent for very long, you've experienced the kind of frustration and discouragement reflected in these comments.

It's true that children can be one of our greatest sources of joy in life. It's also true that they can be one of the greatest sources of pain, frustration, discouragement, and feelings of failure. At times it seems as though the problem is our children. In reality, the problem is not as much our kids as the emotions they bring out in us.

The questions Karen and numerous other parents have asked are: How can we deal with the emotions we experience in response to our children's emotions? Is there any way that we can change what we're beginning to see as a destructive pattern? That's what this final chapter is about.

When we allow our emotions to get out of control, we always end up doing more harm than good. Unhealthy expressions of emotions undermine the very principles we're trying to teach them. Not only do we end up becoming poor role models, we also end up feeling guilty, discouraged, and defeated.

Our ability to help our children develop healthy emotional patterns is directly related to our own ability to model healthy emotional patterns. To put it more simply, emotionally unhealthy parents rarely produce emotionally healthy children. Immature parents rarely produce mature children.

Another consequence is that we give them power over us. At a very early age, kids learn the principle of cause and effect. They learn that doing this or not doing that will almost always evoke a certain response from one of their parents. I've seen children behave in certain ways simply because they get a kick out of seeing Mom or Dad out of control.

When we allow our emotions to control us, our perspective becomes clouded and we are more likely to miss the real issues. We are more likely to react to surface issues rather than addressing the root of the problem. It's easy to become so focused on the intensity of our own feelings that we become blind to the needs of our children.

Another reason this is an important issue for us to address is that parents who haven't learned how to deal with their own emotions are at increased risk of becoming abusive parents. They don't start out this way. I have yet to work with an abusive parent who recalls waking up one morning and saying, "I think I'll become an abusive parent today."

Just the opposite is true. They have no idea when their inability to deal with their own emotional responses becomes a problem. I've worked with many abusive parents who were shocked and appalled by the fact they had hit one of their children. They never dreamed they were capable of this kind of behavior. They couldn't understand how it happened. But slowly, gradually over a period of several years, they slipped into a downward spiral of allowing themselves to be controlled by their emotions. They numbed the inner voice of warning and woke to the reality of being a parent who is out of control.

Karen had experienced this tendency in herself. When she

became frustrated with her children, she would make threats. Initially, her kids responded to her threats. But she rarely followed through on them, and it didn't take long for her children to learn that they didn't have to worry about what Mom said. It would blow over in a couple of hours. In fact, on one occasion she had grounded them for the evening. As she walked by their room, she overheard one of them say, "Don't worry, Mom will chill out before nine."

Because they didn't take her anger seriously, Karen found herself gradually increasing the volume of her voice. She also had to raise the seriousness of the consequences to get a response. Fortunately for Karen and her children, she was able to identify and address the problem before it got out of hand.

As Karen continued to share her concerns, she asked the questions I've heard so many times before. The same questions that at times I have asked myself. "Is there any hope? Can I really change the ways in which I respond to my children?" Fortunately, the answer to both of these questions is yes. Over a period of several weeks, I was able to share seven practical steps with Karen that helped her begin the process of change.

STEPS TO GAINING CONTROL

Step 1. Acknowledge, own, and define the problem.

Someone once said that a problem defined is a problem half-solved. The first and most important step in the change process is to acknowledge to ourselves, to God, and then to one or two others that there is a problem. It is surprising how something that sounds so simple can be so difficult.

Acknowledging the problem to ourselves brings our concerns out of the shadows and into the light. It gives the problem clarity and makes it easier to deal with. As we acknowledge the problem before God, we can admit that this is something we can't handle alone. We can claim promises such as Romans 8:28, Philippians 4:13, and 4:19. You might be surprised how encouraging and energizing it can be to look at your concerns in light of who God is and what He has promised to His children.

When we acknowledge the problem to a couple of trusted

friends, we become accountable. It's one thing to admit we have a problem and ask God for help dealing with it. It's quite another thing to share the problem with friends and ask them not only to pray for us but also to periodically check on us.

After acknowledging that there is a problem, we need to accept responsibility for our problem. One of the first things Adam and Eve did after eating the fruit was to place the responsibility for their action on someone else. Eve blamed the serpent and Adam blamed Eve, and then he blamed God for making her. Since then, our fallen nature looks for someone to blame.

In one of my conversations with Karen she said, "If Jordan would just pick up after himself, I wouldn't get so angry." In some ways that was a true statement. However, in saying that, Karen was placing the responsibility for her emotions on her seven-year-old son.

Step 2. Identify the triggers.

The next step involves identifying the kinds of behaviors that trigger your unhealthy emotional responses. What do I mean by a trigger? *Webster's* defines a trigger as "a stimulus that initiates a physiological or pathological process." Most children have things they can do or say that trigger (or stimulate) a negative emotional response from their parents.

The easiest way to do this is to make a list of your children's behaviors that most often lead to your unhealthy emotional responses. This step sounds so simple and logical. It makes sense. Yet we've worked with many parents who have never focused on this part of the problem and made a list of the factors that make them most vulnerable to an unhealthy expression.

Different situations trigger a different response in each of us. Over the years I've found that the following list represents some of the most common kinds:

- Whining or complaining;
- Talking, yelling, or interrupting when on the phone;
- Not doing something they said they'd do;
- Fighting;
- Name calling;
- Borrowing things without asking;

- Not putting things away after they've borrowed them;
- Being late;
- Talking back or showing disrespect.

In Step 2, Karen was able to clearly identify that Jordan's whining, complaining, and talking back were the major triggers for her unhealthy responses. However, as we discussed some specific situations, Karen made the observation that sometimes these behaviors didn't bother her, but at other times, they drove her over the edge.

Step 3. What makes you more vulnerable?

What Karen was starting to see is that it wasn't just certain of Jordan's behaviors that triggered her anger. There were clearly times when her ability to deal with his normal seven-year-old behavior was better than others. Karen realized that there were factors in her life that made her more vulnerable to responding in ways that hurt rather than ways that healed.

Step 3 involves exploring factors in your own life that make it more likely you will respond negatively. The easiest way to do this is to recall three or four of the most recent times you've responded negatively and then look at those situations in light of the following questions:

1. In the previous 24 to 48 hours, what was going on in your life?

Were you busier than usual?

Were there any crises that took place?

Were there any great successes or failures?

Did you have less sleep or exercise than usual?

2. Did these events take place at a certain time of the week?

I've worked with people who discovered that they were much more vulnerable to *losing it* in the middle of the week when they felt overwhelmed. Others have identified the weekend as their most vulnerable time.

3. Are you more vulnerable at a certain time of the day?

Many parents find they are at greatest risk during the hours preceding the evening meal or right before bedtime. When is your *danger zone?*

4. Were you preoccupied with other problems?

The anxiety that comes from dealing with problems in other

areas of our lives can spill over into our relationships with our children. We have less energy and thus a lower tolerance for frustrating situations.

The vast majority of people we have worked with have been able to identify certain patterns in their unhealthy responses. In Step 3 Karen realized that she was much more vulnerable in the evenings, during the middle of the week. "By the middle of the week, I'm more likely to be exhausted by what I've already done, frustrated by what I haven't gotten done, and discouraged by what I think I need to get done before the weekend. On the weekends, it's easier for me to kick back and relax; but for some reason during the week, I seem to get much more intense. It's like I'm on a treadmill."

By identifying times of increased vulnerability, Karen was able to ask her friends to pray more specifically for her. Her increased awareness also made it easier for her to begin to catch her anger at an early stage.

Step 4. How have I responded in the past? What hasn't worked?

Several years ago, I heard someone say, "It's crazy to find out what doesn't work and then keep doing it." My first response was to laugh, but behind that laugh was the realization that there was some real *craziness* in my life. Certain ways that I approached conflict, communicated with my wife and kids, and dealt with personal issues hadn't worked. But I hadn't changed them.

Many parents suffer from this kind of craziness. We spend years pursuing excellence in responding to situations with our kids that don't work. Our responses didn't work five years ago and they're not working today, yet we keep trying them. One of the greatest resources parents have to help us be more effective is an awareness of what hasn't been effective. Our mistakes and failures are a potential gold mine of information on how we can be more effective.

I grew up in California. I now live in Colorado. Over the years, both states have been major producers of gold. I was interested to learn that there are different ways to mine gold. Much of the gold from the California gold rush came from panning the creeks. You have probably seen pictures of the old miner, bent over the stream with a pan in his hand, looking for little gold nuggets.

In Colorado, the miners had to go deep into the ground and dig for their gold. Once they found gold, they had to go through a special process to extract the gold from the rock. The entire process took a lot of time and effort, but it also produced gold.

In parenting, the *gold* may come in the form of an insight. More often, it comes as a result of the difficult process of digging into our past experiences, looking for patterns, and discovering new ways to deal with old problems.

As Karen worked through Step 4, she realized there were several things that didn't work. One thing that didn't work was to react immediately to the situation. "Whenever I take even a few minutes to think and pray about my response, it seems my response is healthier and more constructive."

Other responses that didn't work for Karen were yelling, threatening, overgeneralizing, labeling, and being sarcastic. They had not produced any positive change. Yet those behaviors comprised 90 percent of her responses to Jordan. Step 4 helped her become clear about what not to do.

What patterns haven't worked for you? Which responses have tended to worsen the problems?

Step 5. What might be more effective responses?

In Step 4 you were able to identify what hasn't worked. Step 5 involves putting together a list of different options. What haven't you tried? What haven't you tried with consistency? What have some other parents done in similar situations? What kinds of responses are more consistent with what you want to model for your children?

Karen read several books on parenting and talked with some of her friends as well as her children's schoolteachers. She was able to develop a two-page list of suggestions. She prayed about them, prioritized them, and prepared to put them into action.

Step 6. Develop a realistic plan.

By the time we reached Step 6, Karen was surprised to find that she was already beginning to see some change. By this time, she had acknowledged, owned, and defined her problem. She had identified the triggers and determined the factors that made her more vulnerable. She had also identified what hadn't worked in the past as well as what might work in the future.

The act of going through the first five steps had significantly increased her awareness, given her more hope, and helped her clarify her prayer life. On a weekly basis, her friends encouraged her by asking how she was doing, what she was learning, and if there were any specific ways in which they could pray for her.

One of the first parts of Karen's plan was to work on developing realistic expectations for herself and for her children. For so many years, she had worked on being the perfect mother. This pursuit of perfection caused her to overcompensate —failure led to guilt and shame, which led to an *I'll do better next time* syndrome. Often this kind of response leads to unrealistic expectations and increased chance of failure. Once the failure occurs there is even more guilt and shame, which produces an even more intense *I'll really do better next time* response, which creates even more unrealistic expectations.

Karen made a commitment to exchanging her pursuit of perfection for a pursuit of growth. Whereas perfection is not an achievable state, at least this side of heaven, growth is a very realistic process. A pursuit of growth not only allows for failures, but we know that if Romans 8:28 is true, then even our failures can be used by God to help us grow. This realization can free us from the overcompensation syndrome.

Karen also decided to clarify what kinds of expectations were realistic for her children. She had a tendency to have similar expectations for both children. She hadn't taken into account age-related developmental differences or the implications of different personality types. These basic insights proved to be of significant help in understanding her children and being able to respond in ways that facilitated clear communication rather than merely increasing frustration.

One of the most important insights Karen made was to see that she needed to retrain herself to pause before dumping on Jordan. Proverbs 14:29 says that the person who is "slow to anger has great understanding." Proverbs 16:32 tells us that the person who is "slow to anger is better than the mighty." In Proverbs 19:11 we are told how this works. It says that "A man's discretion makes him slow to anger." Discretion involves being cautious or reserved in speech and increases our ability to make responsible decisions.

I encouraged her to take a brief time-out before reacting to a potentially explosive situation. This time-out would give her a chance to ponder and pray about her responses. By this time it had become clear to her that there is an enormous difference between reacting and responding. When we react, we are much more vulnerable to allowing our emotions to control us. When we respond, we are much more likely to say and do things that contribute to a solution.

The final part of Karen's plan was to have a new set of responses available to her. Through her prayer, conversations, and readings Karen realized that there were a variety of untried, positive ways to respond to Jordan. However, when she was in the middle of a situation—when she allowed her emotions to get out of control and blur her ability to think clearly—she invariably slipped back into her old response patterns.

The best time to deal with a problem is before it becomes a problem. Karen narrowed down her list of new responses to three and put each one on a 3 x 5 card. Every morning, as part of her prayer time, she asked God for His strength to help her get out of her behavioral rut. Her husband helped her role-play some problem situations so she could have an opportunity to hear herself respond in new ways. This proved to be a valuable exercise for her.

Karen's plan was simple, specific, practical, achievable, and measurable. Her plan went beyond good intentions to specifics. The best news of all is that, over a four-month period, Karen's plan worked.

Step 7. Assess your results and set new goals.

Many people want to be different, but few people want to go through the process of change. Change takes time. It can be frustrating and discouraging. The process of change involves failure. But it is only as we allow God to help us change that we can become the men and women, the moms and dads, that we want to be.

The change process rarely occurs overnight. When you assess your results, it's important to look for the small signs of growth. Three simple ways to measure growth is to look for a decrease in the frequency, intensity, and/or the duration of the unhealthy response.

But keep in mind that you will rarely, if ever, see changes in all three of these areas at the same time. In Karen's situation, she first noticed a decrease in the intensity of her negative responses. Then she noticed that her negative responses were briefer. Finally, she noticed a clear decrease in the frequency of her unhealthy responses.

Karen's realistic plan worked. Her next step was to set a new goal. It was hard work for Karen, but she found that her initial victory produced a new sense of confidence and hope. With God's help, she had become empowered to continue the process of change and growth in becoming a healthier individual as well as a more effective mother.

IN CLOSING

After reading this chapter, you might be saying to yourself, "It can't be that easy." If that is what you're thinking, you're right. The change process is as simple as these seven steps. But it's not easy. I don't think it ever gets easy. But over time, with God's help and a clear commitment on your part, it can become easier than it has been.

ENDNOTES

Introduction
1. Adapted from Oliver, Gary J. and Wright, H. Norman, *When Anger Hits Home* (Moody Press, Chicago, Ill: 1992).

Chapter 1
1. Mains, David, *Healing the Dysfunctional Church Family* (Victor Books, Wheaton, Ill.: 1992), 123.
2. Hart, Archibald D., *Feeling Free* (Fleming H. Revell, Old Tappan, N.J.: 1979), 20.
3. Waters, V., "Therapies for Children: Rational Emotive Therapy" in C.R. Reynolds and T.B. Gutkin (Eds.), *Handbook of School Psychology* (John Wiley and Sons, New York: 1982), 572.
4. Adapted from Bernard, Michael E. and Joyce, Marie R., *Rational-Emotive Therapy with Children and Adolescents* (John Wiley and Sons, New York: 1984), 128.
5. Adapted from Ketterman, Grace and Herbert, *The Complete Book of Baby and Child Care for Christian Parents* (Fleming H. Revell, Old Tappan, N.J.: 1982), 359–60.

Chapter 2
1. Carnegie, Dale, *How to Win Friends and Influence People* (Pocket Books, New York: 1936), 43–44.
2. Swindoll, Charles R., *You and Your Child* (Thomas Nelson, Nashville: 1977), 20.
3. Ibid., 21.
4. Smalley, Gary, *The Key to Your Child's Heart* (Word Books, Waco, Texas: 1984), 63–64.
5. Ginot, Haim G., *Between Parent and Child: New Solutions to Old Problems* (Macmillan Company, New York: 1965), 34–35.
6. Armstrong, Thomas, *In Your Own Way: Discovering and Encouraging Your Child's Personal Learning Styling* (Jeremy P. Tarcher, Los Angeles: 1987), 99–100.
7. Ibid., 100, 102
8. Ibid., 101.
9. Ibid.
10. Olney, Claude W., *Where There's a Will There's an A: Parents Manual* (Chesterbrook Educational Publishers, Inc., Paoli, Pa.: 1989), 21.

Chapter 3

1. Bates, Marilyn and Keirsey, David, *Please Understand Me: Character and Temperament Types* (Prometheus Nemesis, Del Mar, Calif.: 1978).
2. Adapted from Wright, H. Norman, *Power of a Parent's Words* (Regal Books, Ventura, Calif.: 1991), 165–66.
3. Adapted from Buss, Arnold H. and Plomin, Robert, *A Temperament Theory of Personality Development* (John Wiley and Sons, New York: 1975), 237.
4. Neff, LaVonne, *One of a Kind: Making the Most of Your Child's Uniqueness* (Multnomah Press, Portland, Ore.: 1988), 24–26.
5. Adapted from Page, Earle C., *Looking at Type* (Capt, Gainesville, Fla.: 1983).
6. Ibid.
7. Ibid.
8. Ibid.
9. Neff, La Vonne, *One of a Kind: Making the Most of Your Child's Uniqueness* (Multnomah Press, Portland, Ore.: 1988), 58–61.
10. Modified and reproduced by special permission by the publisher, Consulting Psychologists Press, Inc., Palo Alto, Calif. 94306 from Report Form for the Myers-Briggs Type Indicators® by Isabel Briggs Myers. Copyright 1991 by Peter B. Myers and Katharine D. Myers. All rights reserved. Further reproduction is prohibited without the publisher's consent. Myers-Briggs Type Indicator is a registered trademark of Consulting Psychologists Press, Inc.

Chapter 4

1. Adapted from *Parents Magazine*, June 1986, 190.
2. Adapted from Dowling, Colette, "Rescuing Your Child from Depression," January 20, 1992, 47.
3. Adapted from Hofen, Brent Q. and Peterson, Brenda, *The Crisis Intervention Handbook* (Prentice Hall, Englewood Cliffs, N.J.: 1982), 21–39.
4. Adapted from Carter, Dr. William Leo, *Kid Think* (Word, Rapha, Dallas, Texas; 1992), 117–18.
5. Adapted from Flach, Frederick F. and Draghi Edetait, Suzanne, *The Nature and Treatment of Depression* (John Wiley and Sons, New York: 1975), 89–90.
6. Adapted from Carter, Dr. William Leo, *Kid Think* (Word, Rapha, Dallas, Texas: 1992), 129.
7. Ibid., 142.
8. Ibid., 134–35.
9. Ibid., 136.
10. Adapted from Wright, H. Norman, *Helping Your Kids Handle Stress* (Here's Life, San Bernardino, Calif.: 1990), 74–78.

Chapter 5

1. Samalin, Nancy, *Love and Anger: The Parental Dilemma* (Viking Penquin, New York: 1991), 5.
2. Vuchiwich, Samuel, *Starting and Stopping Spontaneous Family Conflicts*, Journal of Marriage and the Family, 49, August 1987: 591–601.
3. Hart, Archibald D., *Stress and Your Child* (Word Publishing, Dallas, Texas: 1992), 110–11.

Chapter 6

1. Adapted from Staudacher, Carol, *Beyond Grief* (New Harbinger Publications, Inc., Oakland, Calif.: 1987), 129–30.
2. Van Ornum, William and Mordock, John B., *Crisis Counseling with Children and Adolescents* (Continuum, New York: 1983), 21–33.
3. Adapted from Rando, Therese A., *Grieving* (Lexington Books, Lexington, Mass.:1988), 200–04.
4. Staudacher, Carol, *Beyond Grief* (New Harbinger Publications, Inc., Oakland, Calif.:1987), 131–38.
5. Ibid., 146–47.
6. Ibid., 151.
7. Adapted from Rando, Therese A., *Grieving* (Lexington Books, Lexington, Mass.:1988), 215–21. And Rando, T.A. (Ed.), *Loss and Anticipatory Grief* (Lexington Books, Lexington, Mass.:1988), 218.
8. Volga, Linda Jane, *Helping a Child Understand Death* (Fortress Press, Philadelphia: 1975), 63–64.
9. Adapted from Rando, Therese A., *Grieving* (Lexington Books, Lexington, Mass.:1988), 218.
10. Adapted from Staudacher, Carol, *Beyond Grief* (New Harbinger Publications, Inc., Oakland, Calif.: 1987), 138–39.

Chapter 7

1. Adapted from (a) Graziano, A.M., DeGiovanni, I.S., and Garcia, K.A., "Behavioral Treatment of Children's Fears: A Review," *Psychological Bulletin,* 1979, 86, 804–30.
(b) Sarafino, E.P., "Children's Fears," in Corsini, R.J. Corsini (Ed.), *Encyclopedia of Psychology* (Vol. 1) John Wiley and Sons, New York: 1984).
(c) Sarafino, E.P. and Armstrong, J.W., *Child and Adolescent Development* (Scott, Foresman, Glenview, Ill.: 1980).
2. Adapted from Sarafino, E.P. and Armstrong, J.W., *Child and Adolescent Development* (Scott, Foresman, Glenview, Ill.: 1980).
3. Adapted from Sarafino, E.P., "Children's Fears," in Corsini, R.J. (Ed.), *Encyclopedia of Psychology* (Vol. 1), John Wiley and Sons, New York: 1984).
4. Ibid., 20–34.
5. Adapted from Kellerman, Jonathan, *Helping the Fearful Child* (W.W. Norton and Co., New York: 1981), 19–20.
6. Adapted from Sarafino, E.P., "Children's Fears," in Corsini, R.J. (Ed.), *Encyclopedia of Psychology* (Vol. 1), John Wiley and Sons, New York: 1984), 36.
7. Ibid., 37.
8. Adapted from Buss, A.H. and Plomin, R., *A Temperamental Theory of Personality Development* (John Wiley and Sons, New York: 1975), 7. And Sontag, L.W. and Wallace, R.I., "Preliminary Report of the Fels Fund: A Study of Fetal Activity," *American Journal of Diseases of Children*, 48, 1934, 1050–57.
9. Adapted from Sarafino, E.P., "Children's Fears," in Corsini, R.J. (Ed.), *Encyclopedia of Psychology* (Vol. 1) (John Wiley and Sons, New York: 1984), 40–41.
10. Ibid., 53.
11. Ibid., 65–66.
12. Adapted from Bandura, "Self-efficacy: Toward a Unifying Theory of

Behavioral Change," *Psychological Review*, 1977, 84, 191–215.

13. Adapted from Sarafino, "Children's Fears," in Corsini, R.J. (Ed.), *Encyclopedia of Psychology* (Vol. 1), (John Wiley and Sons, New York: 1984), 75.

14. Ibid.

15. Braga, J. and Braga, L., *Children and Adults: Activities for Growing Together* (Prentice-Hall, Englewood Cliffs, N.J.: 1976), 262–64.

16. Adapted from Sarafino, "Children's Fears," in Corsini, R.J. (Ed.), *Encyclopedia of Psychology* (Vol. 1) (John Wiley and Sons, New York: 1984), 127.

Chapter 8

1. Adapted from Bernard, Michael E. and Joyce, Marie R., *Rational-Emotive Therapy with Children and Adolescents: Theory Treatment Strategies, Preventative Methods* (John Wiley and Sons, New York: 1984), 156–57. And Harris, Paul L., *Children and Emotion: The Development of Psychological Understanding* (Basil Blackwell, Inc., New York: 1989), 81–105.

2. Lewis, C.S., Kilby, Clyde (Ed.), *Letters to an American Lady* (Eerdmans, Grand Rapids, Mich.: 1967), 97.

3. Adapted from Wilson, Sandra D., *Released from Shame: Recovery for Adult Children of Dysfunctional Families* (InterVarsity Press, Downers Grove, Ill.: 1990). And Bradshaw, John, *Healing the Shame that Binds You* (Health Communications, Inc., Deerfield Beach, Fla.: 1988).

4. Adapted from Ashner, Laurie and Meyerson, Mitch, *When Parents Love Too Much* (Avon Books, New York: 1990), 53.

5. Attributed to Paul Frisch by Karen, Robert, "Shame," *The Atlantic Monthly* (Vol. 269) No. 2, February 1992, 43.

6. Adapted from Kostelnik, Marjorie J., Stein, Laura C., Phipps Whiren, Alice, and Soderman, Anne K., *Guiding Children's Social Development* (South-Western Publishing Co.: 1988), 117.

Chapter 9

1. Hart, Archibald, *Stress and Your Child* (Word Publishing, Dallas, Texas: 1992), 15–16.

2. Miller, Mary Susan, *Childstress* (Doubleday and Co., New York: 1982), 22–23.

3. Adapted from Hart, Archibald, *Stress and Your Child* (Word Publishing, Dallas, Texas: 1992), 46–47.

4. Aiello, John R., Nicosia, Gregory, and Thompson, Donna E., "Psychological, Social and Behavioral Consequences of Crowding on Children and Adolescents," *Social Development*, 50, March 1979, 195–202.

5. *Los Angeles Times* (Section 1), May 16, 1992, 1.

6. Hart, Archibald, *Stress and Your Child* (Word Publishing, Dallas, Texas: 1992), 181.

7. Ibid., 47–50.

8. Kalter, Neil, "Growing Up with Divorce," *The Free Press*, 1990, 66–67.

9. Ibid., 68.

10. Adapted from Youngs, Bettie B., *Stress in Children* (Avon Books, New York: 1985), 55–57.

11. Hart, Archibald, *Stress and Your Child* (Word Publishing, Dallas, Texas: 1992), 245.

12. Meadows, Donald C., Porter, Barbara J., and Welch, David I., *Children Under Stress* (Prentice-Hall, Englewood Cliffs, N.J.: 1983), 10–12.

13. Adapted from Wright, H. Norman, *Helping Your Kids Handle Stress* (Here's Life, San Bernardino, Calif.: 1990), 48–49.

14. Meadows, Donald C., Porter, Barbara J., and Welch, David I., *Children Under Stress* (Prentice-Hall, Englewood Cliffs, N.J.: 1983), 30.

15. Adapted from Saunders, Antoinette, and Remsberg, Bonnie, *The Stress-Proof Child* (New American Library, New York: 1984), 31–32.

Chapter 10

1. Wright, H. Norman, *Helping Your Kids Handle Stress* (Here's Life Publishers, San Bernardino, Calif.: 1989), 32–33.

2. Adapted from Miller, Mary Susan, *Childstress* (Doubleday and Co., Inc., Garden City, N.Y.: 1982), 26–33.

3. Adler, Joseph, "A Lesson Plan for Kid Stress," *Los Angeles Times Magazine,* October 7, 2, 22.

4. Adapted from Wright, H. Norman, *Helping Your Kids Handle Stress* (Here's Life Publishers, San Bernardino, Calif.: 1989), 92–96.

5. Hart, Archibald, *Stress and Your Child* (Word Publishing, Dallas, Texas: 1992), 125–27.

6. Ibid., 66–70.

7. Ibid., 125–27.

8. Ibid., 246.

9. Adapted from Miller, Mary Susan, *Childstress* (Doubleday and Co., Inc., Garden City, N.Y.: 1982), 42–53.

Chapter 11

1. Chase, Betty, *Discipline Them, Love Them* (David C. Cook, Elgin, Ill.: 1982), 60.

2. Narramore, Bruce, *You're Someone Special* (Zondervan Publishers, Grand Rapids, Mich.: 1979), 67.

3. Ibid., 73.

4. Illsley, Jean, Dawson, Clarke and Connie, *Growing Up Again* (Harper and Row, New York: 1989), 17–27.

5. Adapted from *Growing Up Again,* 79–97.

6. Adapted from Leman, Kevin, *Measuring Up* (Dell Publishing, New York: 1988), 41–42.

7. Adapted from Wright, H. Norman, *Power of a Parent's Word* (Regal Books, Ventura, Calif.: 1991), 142–50.

8. Phillips, Debora, *How to Give Your Child a Great Self-Image* (Random House, New York, 1989), 59.

9. Ibid., 87–89.

ADDITIONAL READING

Hart, Archibald, D., *Stress and Your Child* (Word Publishing, Dallas, Texas: 1992).

Hart, Archibald D., *Feeling Free* (Fleming H. Revell, Old Tappan, N.J.: 1979).

Keirsey, David and Bates, Marilyn, *Please Understand Me: Character and Temperaments* (Prometheus Nemesis, Del Mar, Calif.: 1978).

Kroeger, Otto and Thuesen, Janet M., *Type Talk: The Sixteen Personality Types that Determine How We Live, Love and Work* (Delacorte, New York: 1988).

Myers, Isabel B. and Myers, Peter B., *Gifts Differing* (Consulting Psychologists Press, Inc., Palo Alto, Calif.: 1980).

Narramore, Bruce, *You're Someone Special* (Zondervan Publishers, Grand Rapids: 1979).

Neff, La Vonne, *One of a Kind: Making the Most of Your Child's Uniqueness* (Multnomah Press, Portland Ore.: 1988).

Oliver, Gary J. and Wright, H. Norman, *When Anger Hits Home* (Moody Press, Chicago: 1992).

Ward, Ruth M., *Blending Temperaments: Improving Relationships—Yours and Others* (Baker Book House, Grand Rapids: 1988).

Ward, Ruth M., *Self Esteem: A Gift from God* (Baker Book House, Grand Rapids: 1984).

White, Burton L., *The First Three Years of Life* rev. ed. (Prentice Hall, Englewood Cliffs, N.J.: 1990).

Wright, H. Norman, *Helping Your Kids Handle Stress* (Here's Life, San Bernardino, Calif.: 1990).

Wright, H. Norman, *Power of a Parent's Words* (Regal Books, Ventura, Calif.: 1991).